THE RIVERMEN

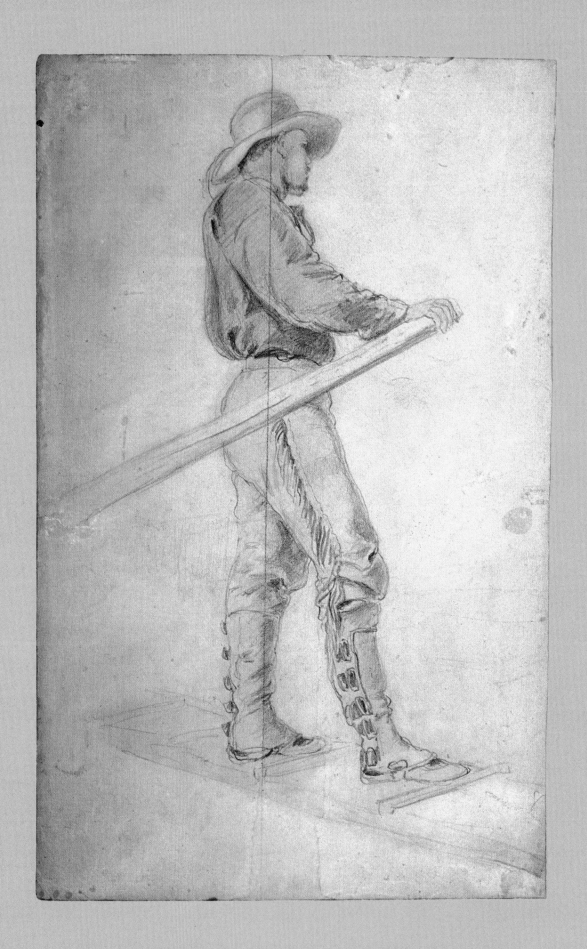

THE RIVERMEN

By the Editors of

TIME-LIFE BOOKS

with text by

Paul O'Neil

TIME-LIFE BOOKS, NEW YORK

Time-Life Books Inc.
is a wholly owned subsidiary of
TIME INCORPORATED

Founder: Henry R. Luce 1898-1967

Editor-in-Chief: Hedley Donovan
Chairman of the Board: Andrew Heiskell
President: James R. Shepley
Vice Chairman: Roy E. Larsen
Corporate Editor: Ralph Graves

TIME-LIFE BOOKS INC.

Managing Editor: Jerry Korn
Executive Editor: David Maness
Assistant Managing Editors: Ezra Bowen,
Dale Brown, Martin Mann
Art Director: Sheldon Cotler
Chief of Research: Beatrice T. Dobie
Director of Photography: Melvin L. Scott
Senior Text Editors: William Frankel, Diana Hirsh
Assistant Art Director: Arnold C. Holeywell
Assistant Chief of Research: Myra Mangan

Chairman: Joan D. Manley
President: John D. McSweeney
Executive Vice President: Carl G. Jaeger
Executive Vice President: David J. Walsh
Vice President and Secretary: Paul R. Stewart
Treasurer and General Manager: John Steven Maxwell
Business Manager: Peter B. Barnes
Mail Order Sales Director: John L. Canova
Public Relations Director: Nicholas Benton

THE OLD WEST

EDITORIAL STAFF FOR "THE RIVERMEN"
Editor: George Constable
Picture Editors: Jean Tennant, Mary Y. Steinbauer
Text Editors: Valerie Moolman, Gerald Simons
Designers: Herbert H. Quarmby, Bruce Blair
Staff Writers: Lee Greene, Kirk Landers,
Robert Tschirky, Eve Wengler
Chief Researcher: June O. Goldberg
Researchers: Jane Jordan, Nancy Miller,
Loretta Britten, Jane Coughran, Thomas Dickey,
Denise Lynch, Vivian Stephens, John Conrad Weiser
Design Assistant: Faye Eng
Editorial Assistant: Lisa Berger

EDITORIAL PRODUCTION
Production Editor: Douglas B. Graham
Assistant Production Editors:
Gennaro C. Esposito, Feliciano Madrid
Quality Director: Robert L. Young
Assistant Quality Director: James J. Cox
Associate: Serafino J. Cambareri
Copy Staff: Eleanore W. Karsten (chief),
Barbara H. Fuller, Gregory Weed,
Florence Keith, Pearl Sverdlin
Picture Department: Dolores A. Littles,
Marianne Dowell, Susan Spiller
Traffic: Carmen McLellan

THE AUTHOR: Paul O'Neil got a first-hand taste of steamboating in the 1930s when, as a collegian, he worked summers aboard Alaska Steamship Company vessels shuttling goods and passengers between Seattle and Alaskan ports. After spending more than a decade as a Seattle newspaperman, he moved to New York in 1944 where he was successively a staff writer for TIME, SPORTS ILLUSTRATED and LIFE before becoming a fulltime freelance in 1973. Since then, he has contributed to special issues of LIFE, to *Atlantic* magazine, and has devoted much time to the research and writing of this book.

THE COVER: The insouciant spirit that early became part of workaday life along the Missouri River was captured by George Caleb Bingham in his 1847 painting, *Lighter Relieving a Steamboat Aground.* One of a series of such idyllic scenes by the artist, who grew up in the river towns of central Missouri, it records a crew of bargemen at ease after removing cargo from the stranded steamer upstream. The frontispiece sketch of a buckskin-garbed riverman at the helm of a flat-bottomed boat was drawn by youthful New York artist William Cary during one of his two extended Missouri voyages, in 1861 and 1874. Cary brought back sketchbooks so crammed with rich detail that he used them during the rest of his 30-year career as a magazine illustrator.

Valuable assistance was provided by the following departments and individuals of Time Inc.: Editorial Production, Michael E. Keene; Library, Benjamin Lightman; Picture Collection, Doris O'Neil; Photographic Laboratory, George Karas; TIME-LIFE News Service, Murray J. Gart.

CONTENTS

High-chimneyed paddle wheelers crowd the St. Louis levee in the 1850s, when steamboating was beginning to hit its stride.

1 | A 3,000-mile waterway west

"A great spiral staircase to the Rockies" was one 19th Century traveler's memorable metaphor for the Missouri, whose tortuous bends led canoeists, keelboaters and eventually steamboatmen from the Mississippi all the way to Fort Benton, Montana—nearly half a mile above sea level and 3,000 miles from the river's mouth.

For generations of explorers and exploiters, the Missouri was the key to the West. It excited the imaginations of 16th Century geographers as a possible avenue to the Orient; later, it provided access to the fur riches that drew the first frontiersmen into the wilderness; and after the Civil War, it conveyed thousands of prospectors to Rocky Mountain gold.

The river's orneriness matched its promises. "The broad current," wrote journalist Albert Richardson in 1857, "is unpoetic and repulsive—a stream of flowing mud studded with dead tree trunks and broken by bars." Yet hundreds of steamboats ran this gauntlet to earn profits that might repay the vessel's entire cost in a single voyage.

Eventually technology overtook the rivermen. Beginning in 1859, railroads began to intersect the Missouri, siphoning off water-borne traffic. By 1890, when the last packet boat departed from the deserted levee at Fort Benton, the only reminders of the steamboat's glory days were river bends with names like Malta, Sultan, Diana and Kate Sweeney—each honoring one of the Big Muddy's paddle-wheeled victims.

The Missouri River constantly challenged pilots by shifting its course within the confines of steep bluffs. In this stretch east of Fort Benton, the river has retreated *(at right)* from the flank of the main trough to form a narrow channel—further constricted by the treacherous sand bar at the left.

Flat-bottomed Mackinaws—like the heavily laden *Last Chance,* about to leave Fort Benton in 1878—provided a cheap alternative to the steamboat for downriver-bound passengers and cargo. After the one-way journey, the makeshift craft were usually ripped apart and sold as lumber.

Last Chance

Four sturdy "mountain boats"—small, shallow-draft stern-wheelers built to run the upper Missouri—rest at the levee of Bismarck, Dakota Territory, in 1877. The elk antlers mounted atop the pilothouse of the steamer *Benton* symbolized its status as the fastest boat in the company fleet.

13

The ramshackle boomtown of Fort Benton, farthest navigable point on the Missouri, appears deceptively sleepy during a low-water spell in 1868. When the river was high, as many as seven steamboats a day might dock to unload cargo for overland conveyance to the Montana gold camps.

REGULAR TUESDAY PASSENGER PACKET,
For LEXINGTON, LIBERTY
AND WESTON, MISSOURI RIVER.

THE NEW, STANCH   BUILT STEAM BOAT

ISABEL:

WM. B. MILLER, Master,

Will leave on TUESDAY, the.................inst., at 5 o'clock, P. M.

Every attention will be paid to the comfort and accommodation of Passengers, and Shippers may rely
upon their freight being carefully handled and promptly delivered. **T. H. LARKIN, Agent.**

FOR MISSOURI RIVER.
MUSICAL LINE

THE NEW AND FAST   PASSENGER STEAMER,

AMAZON:

P. M. CHOUTEAU, Master.   BEN F. CHOUTEAU, Clerk.

Will leave on   the   inst., at   o'clock   M.

For Freight or Passage apply on board.

1854. **FOR MISSOURI RIVER.** 1854.

REGULAR MONDAY PASSENGER PACKET.

THE NEW, ELEGANT   AND SWIFT STEAMER

SAM CLOON,

JOHN McCLOY, MASTER,

Will leave for Jefferson City, Boonville, Glasgow, Brunswick, Miami, Carrollton, Waverly, Bowver, Lexington, Wellington, Camden, Sibley, Richfield, Liberty, Independence, Kansas, Parkville, Fort Leavenworth, Weston, St. Joseph, Savannah, Oregon, Linden, Fort Kansas, Mouth of Platte, Ste. Mary's, Council Bluffs and all other Landings on the MISSOURI RIVER.

On Monday,   inst., at 4 o'clock, P. M.

MISSOURI RIVER PACKET
FOR
LEXINGTON, WESTON AND SAINT JOSEPH.

THE NEW AND   FAST STEAMER,

BANNER STATE,

J. B. HOLLAND, Master,

Will leave on *Sunday 9th*   the *9th* inst.,

At *12* o'clock, *A* M.

Democrat print, St. Louis.

MISSOURI RIVER PACKET.

For Boonville, Lexington, Kansas City and Leavenworth.

WAR EAGLE!

E. F. OWEN, Master.

Will Leave on   at   P. M.

Apply on Board, or to *1858*   Agent.

Atlantic and Mississippi Steamship Company.

FOR KANSAS, LEAVENWORTH, ATCHISON, ST. JOSEPH,
COUNCIL BLUFFS & OMAHA.

Steamer JULIA!

JOS. WIDEN, MASTER,

Leaves   the   at   o'clock,   M.

APPLY ON BOARD OR TO   AGENT.

1854. REGULAR 1854.

MISSOURI RIVER PACKET

THE FAST, STAUNCH   BUILT PASSENGER PACKET

HONDURAS,

L. A. WELTON, Master,

Will run regularly throughout the season between the cities of
SAINT LOUIS AND ST. JOSEPH
LEAVING ST. LOUIS EVERY ALTERNATE THURSDAY, AT 5 O'CLOCK, P. M.,
AND ST. JOSEPH EVERY ALTERNATE WEDNESDAY, AT 10 O'CLOCK, A. M.

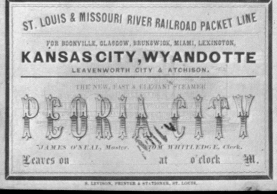

ST. LOUIS & MISSOURI RIVER RAILROAD PACKET LINE
FOR BOONVILLE, GLASGOW, BRUNSWICK, MIAMI, LEXINGTON,
KANSAS CITY, WYANDOTTE
LEAVENWORTH CITY & ATCHISON.

THE NEW, FAST & ELEGANT STEAMER

PEORIA CITY

JAMES O'NEAL, Master.   TOM WHITLEDGE, Clerk.

Leaves on   at   o'clock   M.

S. LEVISON, PRINTER & STATIONER, ST. LOUIS.

Beleaguered voyagers on the Big Muddy

T his night," wrote Nelson Green Edwards, bending by candlelight over a sheet of yellow foolscap, "early Squads of Indians are seen in the High Grass and on the Sides of the Big Hills . . . Lurking & Prowling in a very suspicious manner as if they meditated an attack before morning." Such displays of furtive hostility were not new to the unsettled West by this spring evening of 1869; but the writer had a vantage point far different from that of the wagoneers, cavalrymen, trappers and miners who had encountered the dangers earlier. Edwards, then just 19, was a riverman —the second (or mud) clerk of the Montana-bound Missouri River steamboat *Henry M. Shreve*—and his diary reflected the West as it looked to men who crossed the prairies on the waters of the Big Muddy rather than by land.

Indians seemed like pirates when seen from a boiler deck, and *Shreve*'s crew prepared to repel boarders after anchoring offshore for the night: "24 Musketts was loaded & Caped & Stacked in their Racks. The Brass Howitzer was got in readyness & Loaded with a Shell & Given in Command of John Dynan the Carpenter. Some 8 or 10 in the Cabin & as many more on Deck Stood Guard all night with their Armes all loaded & ready for an attack. Our Fource could have fired 100 guns in 5 minutes."

This communal belligerency had its effect. "There was considerable Stir & Commotion on Board all night but the thing passed off quietly," Edwards noted, "and no blood was spilt on either side." Still, the steamer had been in real danger; and she was only one of hundreds of vessels and Edwards only one of thousands of

rivermen who ascended the Missouri—a 3,000-mile conduit linking St. Louis with the Rockies—during the era of western expansion. Most Americans have been left with the impression that the West was opened almost solely by 1) wagon trains and 2) the railroads, but a prairie schooner carried little cargo and the Iron Horse, for all its final dominance, did not reach the northern Continental Divide until the late 1880s. When weighed in conjunction with its network of westward-reaching tributaries, the Missouri River was, for almost a century, the most important single means of entree into the whole wild and empty subcontinent that lay between the Mississippi and the Pacific Ocean. It was a river that, more than most, meant different things to voyagers in different stratums of time. Men followed it in search of a water route to the Pacific Ocean, mythical kingdoms, furs, precious metals, homesteads, fortunes, adventure and glory.

The Missouri was not, by any means, the only stream that served as a road and channel of commerce for explorers and those who followed them. Rivermen penetrated Louisiana on the Red River of the South and into Oklahoma on the Arkansas; they moved into Iowa on the Des Moines River. The Army used Colorado River steamboats to supply posts in the burning southwestern desert; gold seekers traveled California's Sacramento and San Joaquin rivers in search of the mother lode and rode paddle steamers up the Columbia on their way to new diggings in Idaho and Montana. But none of these matched the Big Muddy in size or geographical import; no other watershed but that of the Mississippi remotely approached its vastness, its wildness and its strategic role in American history of the 19th Century. Early witnesses to its might believed, indeed, that *it* was truly The Father of Waters and that it remained the main stream, after flowing into the Mississippi, which ran south to the Gulf of Mexico. It was

---

In the hotly competitive Missouri River trade, steamboat lines circulated departure cards like these in public places, hoping to win customers away from their rivals.

Unable to ford the river, trappers and their Indian helpers use
a bullboat as a ferry. Such crude, short-haul craft, invented by Indians, were constructed by lashing water-soaked
buffalo hides over a frame of willow saplings. The scene
was recorded by artist Alfred Jacob Miller in the 1830s.

so celebrated in the old emigrant song: *To the West! To the West!/ To the land of the free!/ Where the mighty Missouri rolls down to the sea.*

It was the great watercourse of the prairies — and the longest river on the North American continent: a broad if changeable and dangerous stream which swept from sources on the Continental Divide to a junction with the Mississippi 23 miles north of St. Louis. It led the upstream traveler almost due west across the state of Missouri and then, turning sharply right at the Kansas border, ran north and northwest for almost a thousand miles, dividing Kansas from Missouri and Nebraska from Iowa, bisecting South Dakota and most of North Dakota. After that it headed off due west, roughly parallel with the Canadian border, into the distant reaches of Montana and, finally, traveled west-southwest in a crude and enormous elliptical curve that fetched up under the eastern wall of the Rocky Mountains.

Recklessness was the hallmark of the traveler on the Big Muddy — and of men who invaded the vast wilderness it embraced. The Missouri Valley cradled some of the most warlike of American Indians: Osages, Pawnees, Arikaras, band after band of Sioux, and finally, nearer the Rockies, Assiniboins and the implacable Blackfeet. And the great stream itself demanded hardihood from men who used it. "I have seen nothing more frightful," wrote the French Jesuit Jacques Marquette when he and his fellow explorer Louis Jolliet approached the point at which the Missouri — then at the height of its June rise in 1673 — poured its yellow flood into the Mississippi. "A mass of large trees enters with branches interlocked — a floating island. We could not, without great danger, expose ourselves to pass across."

The river rose twice a year. The first period of high water began in April when the spring rains and prairie snowmelt raised the levels of its tributaries, often drowning the main valley under endless vistas of hurrying brown water. The second rise occurred in either May or June when the sun began melting the snow fields of the Rockies. Thousands and thousands of uprooted trees, hung up on bars in low water, were released like javelins when the water level rose, and the river became charged with floating logs. Thousands more of the trees grew waterlogged, sank at the heavy root end, and hung in the river, some motionless, some rising and falling in the current forming a great, hidden abatis upon

Boatable passages through the wilderness

Though the Missouri River was regarded with fear and awe by early French explorers, American rivermen turned it into a broad road to riches, the main artery in a 12,000-mile network of ready-made pathways to the densest concentration of fur-bearing animals in North America. Yet this vast watershed was only one of many portals to the West and its incredible wealth. In all, more than 20,000 miles of rivers and tributaries lay between the Mississippi and the Pacific Ocean, and in one fashion or another the rivermen found ways to exploit these corridors.

Light-draft vessels like dugout canoes and bullboats were useful on the Platte and other shallow channels; large freighters such as the keelboat, flatboat and Mackinaw, capable of hauling 10 tons or more, plied the Yellowstone, the Missouri and other major waterways.

The steamboat joined the flotilla in 1819 when the Mississippi side-wheeler, introduced eight years before, appeared on the Missouri. Drawing six feet of water and seriously underpowered, the first steamers were largely limited to the deep lower river. Changes widening the beam and lessening the draft gradually extended the vessels' range on the upper river in the 1850s. Finally, in 1859, a true Missouri riverboat came into being—a powerfully engined stern-wheeler that could carry up to 350 tons, while drawing only 31 inches of water over the shallow, ever-shifting bars.

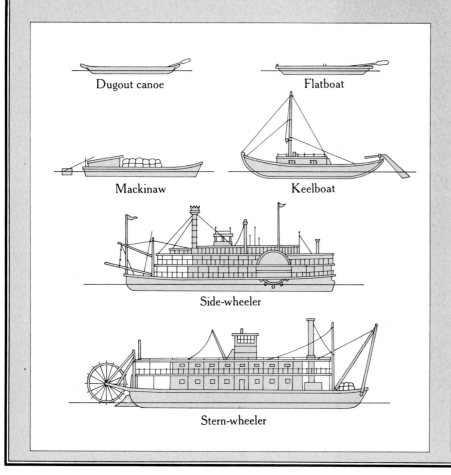

Dugout canoe

Flatboat

Mackinaw

Keelboat

Side-wheeler

Stern-wheeler

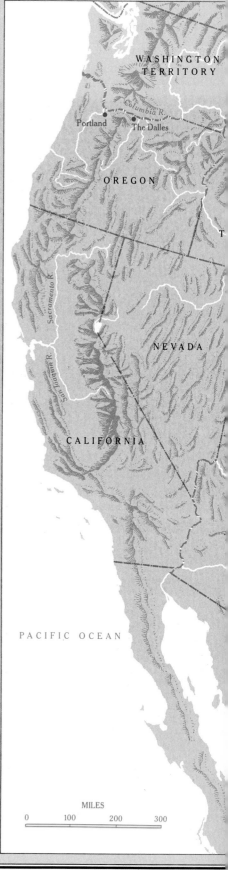

WASHINGTON TERRITORY

Columbia R.

Portland   The Dalles

OREGON

Sacramento R.

San Joaquin R.

NEVADA

CALIFORNIA

PACIFIC OCEAN

MILES

0   100   200   300

LAKE WINNIPEG

CANADA

Milk R.
Poplar R.

Fort Benton
Camp Cooke
Great Falls
DAUPHIN RAPIDS
Cow Island
Fort Buford
Helena
MONTANA TERRITORY
Fort Union
Fort Berthold
ree Forks
Fort Stevenson
Musselshell R.
BIG BELT MTS.
Yellowstone R.
Fort Abraham Lincoln
Bismarck
Fort Rice
POMPEYS PILLAR
Tongue R.
Powder R.
Grand R.
Bighorn R.
BIGHORN MTS.
DAKOTA TERRITORY
LAKE SUPERIOR

MICHIGAN

MINNESOTA

WISCONSIN

LAKE MICHIGAN

ROCKY MOUNTAINS

BLACK HILLS
Cheyenne R.
Fort Sully
Fort Pierre
Fort Thompson
Vermillion R.

WYOMING TERRITORY
Niobrara R.
Fort Randall
Yankton
Sioux City
IOWA

ke City
North Platte R.
NEBRASKA
Missouri R.
Des Moines R.

TORY
Platte R.
Omaha
Council Bluffs
Charlton R.
INDIANA
Cincinnati

UTAH TERRITORY
Nebraska City
ILLINOIS

Colorado R.
COLORADO TERRITORY
St. Joseph
Fort Leavenworth
Westport Landing
Independence
Lexington
St. Charles
St. Louis
Louisville
Ohio R.
FALLS OF THE OHIO

Jefferson City
Osage R.
KANSAS
MISSOURI
KENTUCKY

PUBLIC LAND
TENNESSEE

NEW MEXICO TERRITORY
INDIAN TERRITORY
ARKANSAS
Tennessee R.

Red R.
Arkansas R.
Mississippi R.

MISS.
ALABAMA

TEXAS
Natchez

LOUISIANA

Rio Grande
New Orleans

MEXICO

GULF OF MEXICO

which whole fleets of vessels might impale themselves.

Vast areas of the Missouri froze over in winter, and the first flood often littered itself with grinding floes. The open country through which the river passed was subject to tornadoes, violent thunderstorms, fierce gales and, along river bottoms, to sand storms as thick as those of the Sahara. Prairie fires could blister the paint of vessels that were forced close to the bank by the current. Dense clouds of mosquitoes, bred in the stagnant ponds of old meander channels, were a constant plague. And if a traveler happened to pitch camp ashore, he was likely to discover yet another peril; as one veteran riverman of the pre-steam era noted, "Travelers have often discovered that the bank was sinking, allowing little time to jump into the boat before the seemingly solid ground has vanished before their eyes."

The Missouri remained a critical route, nevertheless, for travelers going beyond the Mississippi. Its great northwestern arc not only led on to the Rockies, but enclosed an enormous system of tributaries; these streams —which watered more than half a million square miles of the Dakotas, Nebraska, Montana, Wyoming and Colorado—opened land routes to almost every other corner of the West. The longest and most usefully sited of the tributary trails lay along the Platte, which conducted the traveler 300 miles west across the grasslands of Nebraska and then, dividing, offered him a route to Colorado and another to the southern Wyoming plateau. It was followed by emigrants heading for the lush Pacific Northwest, by Mormons bound for the Valley of the Great Salt Lake, and by most of the forty-niners pursuing California's golden dream. Two hundred miles below the juncture of the Platte and the Missouri was the head of another major route across the wilderness — the Santa Fe Trail, traveled by throngs of traders and emigrants from 1821 onward. The way west, thus, really began on the Missouri.

Before the age of steam, men paid prodigious prices in physical energy to invade the Big Muddy. Cunning, luck and constant manhandling were needed to get the boats they used through the river's shifting, obstruction-infested bars and channels. Indians rode the Missouri in "bullboats" — circular, clumsy little craft made by stretching the hide of a buffalo bull (which tended to leak less than the hide of a female animal) over a framework of willow branches. But these little coracles could only float small loads across streams or down short stretches of the big river, and they were far less useful than the sharp-prowed American Mackinaws later constructed by white settlers. The Mackinaws were flat-boats up to 70 feet long, which could be quickly slapped together from whipsawed lumber and—given maneuverability by rowers and by a steersman with a big oar at the stern—could float tons of cargo downstream. However, Mackinaws could not be worked against the current, and the long upriver voyages were

negotiated in but two kinds of craft: dugout canoes and graceful keelboats.

Keelboats ran as much as 70 feet in length, were from 15 to 18 feet in beam, and boasted a roofed, midships cabin flanked, on either side, by a narrow, cleated walkway on which crewmen labored in poling the vessel upstream. There were seats for oarsmen—from six to 12 of them—forward of this enclosed storage space. A small brass cannon was usually mounted on the keelboat's bow and its captain stood atop the cabin, aft, to shout commands and handle a steering oar which was fixed at the stern. The keelboat also had a mast which not only took a sail but acted as the point of attachment for a long rope, or "cordelle." Since loaded craft of this type were often dragged when they could not be rowed, poled or sailed, crewmen used the cordelle to tow the keelboat as they waded up to their knees—or necks—in shallows or lurched through brush along the bank. The stalwarts who manned the boats were mostly of French extraction; except for one brief interim pe-

Paying the price of a risky upriver trip at low-water season, the 78-ton stern-wheeler *Expansion* lies grounded on a Yellowstone sand bar. The boat was freed by off-loading passengers and cargo. Once the craft was lightened the river's powerful current was able to wash away the silt beneath.

26

2 | The great fur rush upriver

In 1806, when pathfinders Meriwether Lewis and William Clark returned to St. Louis after their epic exploration of the Missouri and points west, they reported exultantly: "We view this passage across the continent as affording immence advantages to the fir trade."

Their glowing tales of the beaver supply on the upper Missouri and in the Rockies instantly set off a frenzied fur rush up the Big Muddy. Entrepreneurs and adventurers of every description attempted the river in keelboats or in dugouts made from giant cottonwood logs. Rowing, sailing and—more often than not—hauling their clumsy craft against the current, they generally expended an entire summer in attaining the upper reaches of the stream. But once a trapper arrived in beaver country he could expect to harvest about 120 pelts per year—worth the then-tidy sum of $1,000 or so back East.

There was no artist on hand to record the beauties and hazards of their first journeys. But in 1833, a peripatetic German naturalist, Prince Maximilian, boarded the keelboat *Flora* to explore the upper river, unchanged since the early days of the fur trade. With him was a Swiss artist, Karl Bodmer, who faithfully recreated life on the Missouri as it was before the age of steam.

The keelboat *Flora,* anchored near a Gros Ventre camp on the Missouri, is besieged by Indians eager to barter beaver pelts for brandy.

On the way downstream with a load of furs, traders ground their craft on a bank and disembark for the evening meal. Before settling in for the night, wilderness veterans usually sent scouts into the woods to check for hostile Indians.

A cavalcade of Mandan Indians crosses the frozen Missouri after a midwinter visit to Fort Clark, a major trading post sited on a bluff near present-day Bismarck. The ice could easily support them: it formed early in November, reached a thickness of four feet, and did not break up until April.

49

In artist Bodmer's dramatic masterpiece, trappers receive an unpleasant — but not uncommon — surprise: a pair of ravenous grizzlies has discovered the meat cache left by an advance contingent of hunters, leaving little but bones for the landing party to take back with them to their keelboat.

50

Having come 1,000 miles up the Mississippi from New Orleans in 1763, fur trader Pierre La Clede extends his hand in friendship to an Osage

chief at the spot where St. Louis would rise. This re-creation of the city's founding was painted by German artist Charles Wimar a century later.

The fur rush was at its peak in the early
1830s when Karl Bodmer made this study
of a beaver den on the Missouri. Factories
in England and Germany turned the pelts
into top hats that sold for about $10 each.

without realizing that these were usually passed from
tribe to tribe. The process of transmission not only produced a gradual alteration of substance, but — since each
proclaimant gave his tale an immediacy it did not usually deserve and assumed it had sprung into being not
far from where he had heard it — also produced a fore-
shortened idea of time and distance. Frenchmen, there-
fore, had no way of knowing that the "ill-smelling inland
sea" was probably Lake Winnipeg, a large body of
water, edged by mud flats and marshes, in what is now
Manitoba. It lay nowhere near the Pacific Ocean, and
the nearest point of the Missouri was 300 miles to the
southwest of the lake.

Indians tended, while reworking geography, to en-
dow the wilderness with all sorts of wondrous civili-
zations akin to the one that had lured Coronado to
Kansas. In the early 18th Century, for instance, the
French explorer Étienne Venyard, Sieur de Bourgmont,
ventured a few hundred miles up the lower Missouri in
full expectation of verifying Indian reports of white
dwarfs who had eyes set out an inch from their noses,
lived on the inland sea, trafficked in rubies and wore
boots studded with gold. Although Bourgmont failed to
meet them, he remained convinced that they retreated
deeper into the West on hearing of his approach and
that they would be found in due course.

White men sometimes started such rumors themselves — although their imaginings usually met with
much greater suspicion. Such was the fate of one Math-
ew Sagean, a French marine who delivered himself of a
wild flight of fancy while serving at Brest on the Britta-
ny peninsula in 1701. Sagean's tale was admittedly
somewhat dated; he swore that he had been captured
by English pirates after service with Robert Cavelier,
Sieur de la Salle — an explorer who came upon the
mouth of the Missouri nine years after Marquette and
Jolliet. But now he felt duty-bound to reveal secrets
that he had kept locked in his breast during 20 years

among "heretical foreigners," as he called the English.

He and some French companions, Sagean said, had paddled upstream for about 500 miles and then carried their canoes overland an unspecified distance — meeting lions and tigers en route. Finally they entered the great nation of the Acanibas, whose king lived inside walls of solid gold. Sagean was not fond of the Acanibas: their heads had been made narrow and hideous as the result of being pressed between boards in infancy; their women had huge ears; and their taste in music, in his opinion, left a good deal to be desired. Still, they sent caravans of gold to Japan and received iron and steel in payment. They were hospitable: girls who refused to bed down with the Frenchmen were dispatched with daggers. They had many parrots and monkeys. And they gave away gold bars; Sagean claimed he had carried off 60 of these bars when he left (amid "terrific howlings" by his hosts) but had, alas, lost them all to his monstrous English captors.

No one in the New World was inclined to act on Sagean's inventive report, even though the Comte de Ponchartrain — one of Louis XIV's ministers and a more credulous man than most — shipped Sagean all the way to Louisiana to circulate his tale. But the desire to find a water route to the Pacific — hopefully one less strenuous than the eastward-flowing Missouri — remained as keen as ever. Ironically, it was the search for an alternative stream that finally led white men to the upper Missouri at last.

In 1727, a Quebec-born fur trader, Pierre Gaultier de Varennes, Sieur de la Vérendrye, heard the old story of a west-flowing connection with the Pacific from a new source — from Indians at Lake Nipigon, 35 miles north of Lake Superior. He pursued it so doggedly as to become one of Canada's greatest explorers. La Vérendrye was a blunt, purposeful patriot who served in the French Army (incurring nine wounds) during the War of the Spanish Succession and who devoted himself wholeheartedly to the fortunes of the government's fur operations after returning to his native Quebec. He spent seven years cultivating the Crees and Assiniboins, and building a series of trading posts (Fort St. Pierre, Fort St. Charles, Fort Maurepas) north of the border of present-day Minnesota.

La Vérendrye sent 30,000 beaver pelts back to Montreal each year, but he paid a tragic personal price for unsealing the riches of the wilderness. In 1736, his oldest son, with 20 other men, was murdered by Sioux on an island in Lake of the Woods. The Indians decapitated their victims and, in an eerie gesture of contempt, wrapped their heads in beaver skins. La Vérendrye nevertheless pressed on, determined to find the river described by Indian informants.

He built Fort Rouge at the site of Winnipeg in 1738 and that November — properly positioned at last and with an escort of 400 friendly Assiniboins — marched across the frozen prairies and came upon the upper Missouri at the Mandan villages near present-day Bismarck, North Dakota. Just as he had hoped, the stream flowed southwest (though only because of a vast local bend). Unfortunately, his interpreter decamped before he could wring any detailed geographical information from the Mandans. He was not impressed by what he learned from that tribe's use of sign language: they told him they lived at the center of the world. But it was clear enough that the Pacific lay much farther away than he thought. He retreated to Canada in discouragement and declining health prevented him from resuming the search.

However, the upper Missouri had at last been seen by a white man, and others soon drifted toward its waters — Gallic canoemen coming from the trading posts that La Vérendrye had established to the north. No white men ever blended so successfully with the tribal cultures of the Missouri Valley as did these *"coureurs de bois"* — literally, "runners of the woods" — who rode the Missouri in wooden dugouts to seek furs, savor the wilderness and take wives among the *sauvages* (a term that, for all their acceptance of Indian ways, they stubbornly refused to abandon). There is no way of knowing how far upstream they went; these adventurers were illiterates who kept no records. But it is known that two of La Vérendrye's surviving sons returned to the river in the spring of 1742 and traveled to the west of it for months, encountering various Plains Tribes. The two wanderers probably saw the Black Hills and, quite possibly, a front range of the Rockies.

The world paid them little heed. England soon swallowed French Canada, and the Dakota prairies swallowed the lead tablet the brothers left behind to claim for France all that they had seen. (The tablet was rediscovered in 1913 by a 14-year-old Fort Pierre,

Trappers unload pelts to be exchanged for gunpowder, whiskey and other staples at Bellevue, a compound of traders' cabins and storehouses near

present-day Council Bluffs, Iowa. The post, given a pastoral air by artist Karl Bodmer, was built in 1810 by St. Louis-based fur merchants.

An affectionate tribute to a vanishing breed

The hardy boatmen who fought the Missouri by muscle rather than steam were on duty 16 hours a day and had to subsist, much of the time, on pork, lima beans and rotgut whiskey. Yet the job never lacked for recruits, since it offered moments of camaraderie that more than made up for the hours of toil. This placid, sunlit side of the early rivermen's lives was a source of endless fascination to George Caleb Bingham, a self-taught frontier artist who grew up in Franklin, Missouri, a river town at the head of the Santa Fe Trail.

When Bingham began to work in 1845 on the canvases shown here and on the following pages, the Big Muddy was in a state of radical transition. The keelboat, long the prime means of moving bulk cargo upstream, was near extinction, running only on the shoal-plagued stretch of water between the mouth of the Yellowstone and Fort Benton. The rest of the river — and the future — belonged to the steamboat.

But the day of the muscle-powered vessel was not quite over. Mackinaws and flatboats still ranked as the cheapest form of downstream transport: a Mackinaw able to haul 15 tons of freight could be hired — crew and all — for as little as $2 a day. Despite the complaint of fur-trade memorialist Washington Irving that "the march of mechanical invention . . . is driving everything poetical before it," Bingham's carefree boatmen remained a fixture on the Missouri well into the 1870s.

The young crew and pipe-smoking master of a small flatboat wait for a steamer to buy their load of firewood. These "wood boats" were among the last muscle-powered craft to disappear from the Missouri River.

The crucial moment in a card game between two flatboatmen draws a pair of kibitzers to the contest, leaving a single crewman to handle

navigational chores. Gambling and drinking were steady fare on a flatboat voyage — making the craft among the worst insurance risks on the river.

Three opportunistic flatboatmen take their ease on a bank of the Big Muddy and prepare for their evening meal after retrieving the cargo

of a steamboat sunk by a snag *(background)*. Such salvage operations were a lucrative part of the flatboat's role throughout the era of steam.

Loaded to capacity, the stern-wheeler *Rosebud* churns upstream under a full head of steam during a high-water period in the 1880s.

3 | "Steamboat acomin'"

Steam power — scarcely tamed when it came to the Missouri in 1819 — was the force that enabled the river to realize its destiny as a life line to the Rockies. By the late 1830s the lower river was raucous with paddle wheelers, some resembling the Mississippi side-wheelers that one skipper hailed as "the most beautiful creation of man."

After the Civil War, a distinctive form of riverboat began to chuff up the Big Muddy to the welcoming shouts of "steamboat acomin'!" It was a no-frills stern-wheeled workhorse especially designed for upper-river voyages. Small and far from sturdy, these boats lasted about eight years on the average, and betrayed their hard lives visibly. One traveler wrote of their "cracked roofs and warped decks, especially adapted to the broiling of passengers in fair weather and drenching them in foul."

Yet during low-water periods, when channels were only waist-deep in spots, the little vessels could carry 200 tons, and they could double that if conditions permitted another foot of draft. Often patched up, sometimes with parts salvaged from wrecks, the doughty stern-wheelers were still busy on the Big Muddy when the glittering side-wheel packets were nearing oblivion.

A pleasing sight on the Missouri was an elegant side-wheeler like *Silver Bow,* shown at Fort Leavenworth in 1869. Although passengers admired her looks, luxury and speed, most steamboatmen chose the homely stern-wheelers, in good part because they were not as vulnerable to snags.

The proud old stern-wheeler *F. Y. Batchelor* had been sunk, raised and converted into a stripped-down freight carrier when this picture was taken at Bismarck in the 1880s. A few years earlier, she set the upstream record from Bismarck to Fort Buford: 307 miles in 55 hours, 25 minutes.

"Fill her fireboxes, I want more steam!"

The Big Muddy thrust its tide against a wide promontory above Lexington, Missouri, during the spring flood of 1852 and reacted—on being turned aside—by feeding an angry, ice-littered brown torrent down the channel that boats used to round the bend on their way upstream. The side-wheel steamer *Saluda*—Captain Francis T. Belt, owner and master—was firing hard in consequence as she drew abreast of the town on Wednesday, April 7, and prepared to skirt the point of land ahead. But her double-engine, double-boiler power plant was just not capable of coping with the ugly water into which she thrust her bow. She hurried into it time and time again, hung in the current with her exhaust banging violently and with chunks of ice thudding against her hull, and was each time slowly washed astern. Captain Belt fell back on Lexington in the end, nosed the side-wheeler against a wharf, and tied her up.

The boat's staterooms and lower deck were jammed with Mormon immigrants, most of them from England and Wales, who were bound for Council Bluffs and the head of the long trail to the Salt Lake Valley. Cold, crowding and enforced idleness made them restive. They complained.

Belt took the side-wheeler out into the stream again the following day and was driven back once more. *Saluda's* machinery was old and worn; she had been snagged and sunk two years before, but Belt—having bought her for a very low price after she was raised and patched—hoped to make big profits from her. Now he

was outraged at the demeaning role he was being forced to play before his grumbling passengers and before an increasingly interested gallery on the shore. On April 9, Good Friday, he resolved to force progress by beating *Saluda* as one might beat a balky horse that refused to pull its weight.

He walked into the engine room shortly after 7 o'clock in the morning and demanded to know how much more pressure her boilers would stand. "Not a pound more than she's carrying now," said the second engineer, Josiah Clancey, according to a subsequent newspaper account of the incident. Belt ordered water injection shut off and the safety valve locked down. "Fill her fireboxes up. I want more steam. I'm going to round that point or blow her to hell trying." He climbed up to the hurricane deck, pulled the clapper of the boat's bell and then—after a Lexington butcher obligingly cast off her lines and the mate and three deck hands poled her bow away from the shore—called for slow speed ahead.

Saluda's paddles splashed through two revolutions and the boilers exploded. The hull disintegrated forward of the engine room and half the upper works went skyward—accompanied by tumbling human bodies and the two iron chimneys—in a great, concussive blossoming of steam, bales, splinters, boiling water and wreckage from the cabins. Captain Belt's lacerated corpse took a high, parabolic course inland with the bell on which he had placed one elbow in the second before death; both landed high on a bluff above the river and rolled downhill together, the bell clanging wildly. A 600-pound iron safe, the boat's watchdog (which had been chained to its door) and second clerk Jonathan F. Blackburn were flung high in the air; they came to rest near one another 200 yards from the river. A local butcher, ashore, was dismembered by a flying boiler flue. A brick house nearby collapsed under the impact

Early steamboats on the Missouri followed no set schedules, but by the 1850s burgeoning passenger traffic spawned a multitude of lower-river packet companies like the K Line—a two-boat, 270-mile operation that advertised fixed departure times.

The skies boil with smoke as St. Louis burns on the night of May 17, 1849. Fire broke out on the steamer *White Cloud,* spread from vessel to vessel along the crowded levee, then ignited adjacent buildings. Twenty-three steamboats and 15 city blocks were razed in the conflagration.

of another chunk of boiler iron. The two pilots were blown into the river with pieces of the wheelhouse and never seen again.

A curious silence followed the deafening roar of the explosion. But a sound of screaming soon began under piles of wreckage on the after portion of the hull—which sank rapidly near the bank. Townspeople, rushing to the river, found—as the *St. Joseph Gazette* reported —"the mangled remains of other human beings scattered over the wharf, and human blood, just warm from the heart, trickling down the banks and mingling with the water of the Missouri River. Groans, shrieks and sobs, mingled with the plaintive wailings of helpless babes, carried grief and desolation to the hearts of those who were exerting themselves to relieve the sufferers. One wounded child called, 'Mother! Father!' But they had gone to the land of the spirits and it was left alone in the world a helpless orphan."

More than 100 bodies were recovered, and about the same number were believed to have washed down the river. Only about 50 of the people who had been aboard survived.

Saluda was long remembered. Her bell was carried to the nearby town of Savannah and placed in the belfry of the Christian Church. Lexington families adopted her orphaned children and raised them—far from England and Wales, far from the Great Salt Lake and Mormonism—as their own. Most of the children lived the rest of their lives in the town.

The disaster at Lexington was the worst in the history of steam navigation on the Missouri River. *Saluda* was representative, nevertheless, of every paddle steamer that operated on the Big Muddy. Like all such vessels, she offered a matchless boon of mechanized ease, yet engaged in a constant flirtation with sudden violence: Missouri steamers blew up by the dozen and sank by the hundreds. Still, excesses of this kind were only to be expected of an instrument that was capable of bringing about a revolution in a world that had known only muscle, animal, wind and water power since the beginning of time.

Two influences—Western rivers and Western builders —produced a boat different from any other ever before known: a ramshackle, flat-bottomed, multitiered structure that was designed to slide over the water rather than to move through it, and that had the most powerful, as well as the crudest, simplest and most dangerous engines then known to man. It was a wasteful device. Its Ohio Valley builders did what little they could to correct this trait, but they embraced wastefulness as a kind of overall philosophy even while doing so. They were quick to recognize the forests along riverbanks as vast, handy sources of cheap energy. And since they valued speed, power and performance over efficiency (or safety), their boats burned cordwood as extravagantly as subsequent American machines would burn gasoline or electricity.

The builders also favored lightweight construction so that the boat, plying shallow rivers, would draw as little water as possible. To save weight, the decks, floor timbers, bulkheads and upper works were made of pine or poplar rather than sturdier—but heavier—oak. A Council Bluffs newspaperman, with tongue only halfway in cheek, said that a Western steamer was put together out of "wood, tin, shingles, canvas and twine, and looks like the bride of Babylon." But the ungainliness of the craft was worth it: such a vessel might have a draft of as little as 14 inches.

The steamer's light construction and gargantuan appetite for fuel forced captains and pilots to become the servants as well as the masters of vessels on the Big Muddy. The Missouri pilot was confronted with a constant dilemma as soon as he steamed into the upper valley: trees were scarce along great stretches of river, but a prodigal use of wood was mandatory in surmounting the bars and rapids with which his vessel was forced to cope. Pilots had to gauge progress with a hard fact in mind: they dared not run out of fuel before reaching some stream-fed side valley where trees did grow or before coming upon a bar where "racks" of driftwood had collected. All tried to find some such source of wood before tying up for the night. Their long-suffering roustabouts then were given the task of cutting it by the light of flickering pine knots and bringing aboard a supply calculated to ensure hours of steady steaming on the following day.

The steamboat's frail construction, meantime, forced pilots into an endless preoccupation with matters riskier than the fuel supply—and into moments of decision during which the fate of the vessel and all aboard could depend on their coolness at the wheel and their judgment

The flowing script of the clerk of the mountain boat *Black Hills* notes the purchase of 10 cords — or 1,280 cubic feet — of fuel at a woodyard on the Yellowstone. Steamboats usually made two such stops a day.

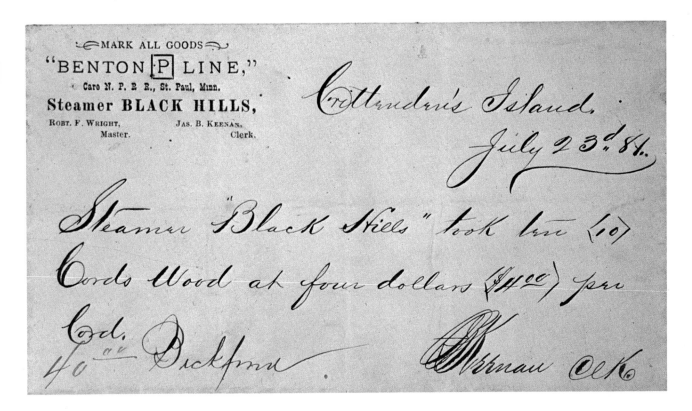

in ringing commands to the engine room. Light construction allowed steamers to surmount sand bars and conquer low water, but it left them at the mercy of rock reefs, snags, high winds and ice in their voyages to the mountains. With its limitations, thus, the steamboat itself was as responsible as the awful river for creating pilots who emerged as the best in America. And, indeed, while pilots were popular heroes on all the Western waters, none held themselves in such high regard as those who served on the Missouri; they considered themselves princes of their profession, commanded salaries as high as $1,500 a month, and made no secret of their condescending view of counterparts on the Ohio and the Mississippi.

They were not without their quota of eccentrics. There was Joe Oldham, for instance, who wore kid gloves in the wheelhouse, kept a diamond-encrusted watch slung around his neck, and was famous for his highhanded dealings with his employers. Summoned at the last minute to take over one steamer's helm, he delayed the vessel's departure for a full 24 hours by first spending the morning demanding (and eventually getting agreement to) a fee of $1,000 for a single week's

trip and then the afternoon and evening at a previously scheduled picnic ashore with friends so dear that he could not bear to disappoint them. "Silent Ben" Jewell —one of the most garrulous men ever born—saw Indians behind every tree, solemnly reported them after every watch, and claimed to have escaped the James gang by swimming across the river with a half million in silver coins in his pockets. But both Jewell and Oldham could take a steamboat through dangerous water, and that was all that was asked of them—or, indeed, of Jacques Desiré, a French-speaking, Louisiana-born black who was a respected Missouri pilot even prior to the Civil War.

A pilot had to memorize the Big Muddy's endless bars, bends, rapids and chutes—and also know the cliffs, dead trees, clearings, cabins, hills and outcroppings at which a steamer was aimed when negotiating them. He had to be capable of deciding, very quickly, whether any landmarks had been washed away or had changed in appearance since he had last looked for them through the windows of his wheelhouse. The principal channel of the Missouri shifted unpredictably on an unstable riverbed, and its periods of receding water

Farfetched gadgets that sank without a trace

In their efforts to build a better steamboat for the shallow rivers of the West, inventors occasionally strayed into the realm of pure wackiness. One of the best known of these errant creators was Abraham Lincoln, who took time from his law practice in 1849 to patent an "Improved Method of Lifting Vessels over Shoals."

Inspired by the old river trick of shoving boxes and barrels under a stranded boat to float it free, Lincoln designed a set of bellows-like "expansible buoyant chambers" to be carried alongside a steamer just above the water line. When the boat entered shoal water, the chambers—made of waterproofed material and perforated at the top—would be expanded by the downward movement of stout poles, filling them with air and presumably giving the vessel a timely boost.

Despite the future President's enthusiasm for his brainchild, no steamer ever used it—possibly because the weight of the contraption was likely to create the sort of problem it was meant to avert. However, it was less farfetched than some shallow-water panaceas. In 1836, for example, a nautical heretic, Gideon Hotchkiss, had the idea of attaching a spiked wheel—described as a "Pedestrian, Traction, Repulsion, Perambulating or Anchor Wheel"—to the bottom of boats so that they could roll along the riverbed in low water. Fifteen years later, a certain William Storm called for the replacement of paddle wheels with a pair of long, cleated belts of "India-rubber, canvas, gutta-percha, sole-leather, or other fit flexible material." A boat so equipped, boasted Storm, would whiz through shallow water faster than a locomotive.

Not all inventors felt that the steamboat was the last word in river travel. In 1828, a dreamer with the promising name of Hull Chase patented a wind-powered side-wheeler. He claimed that a giant propeller mounted atop the boat and linked to the paddle wheels by gears would permit excellent progress into the teeth of the wind. Unfortunately, fact did not coincide with theory, though the wind might have produced some motion when blowing from other angles.

When it came to getting back to basics, no one excelled Samuel Heintzelman. He focused on a specific problem: the fact that rivers often impeded cavalrymen chasing Indians. His solution, patented in 1857, was the essence of simplicity: inflatable saddlebags. With them, he said, horse and rider could effortlessly float across the water. And he even threw in an instant refinement: that cavalrymen put on "waterproof pantaloons with feet" so that they would not have to suffer the discomfort of getting wet.

A model of Lincoln's invention features vertical spars that could be lowered by pulleys to inflate "buoyant chambers" carried beside the hull.

were far more extreme than those that pilots encountered on other rivers.

If the water level was high and the moon full, a boat might run at night; the Missouri, with its load of silt, reflected moonlight better than the Mississippi. Usually, however, the prudent pilot tied up at nightfall—unless a landing lay only a mile or so ahead. Steamers often attempted to negotiate such a short stretch of water in the dark after sending the mate ahead to mark the channel. He performed this rite by affixing lighted candles (in cylindrical paper shields) to pieces of scrap lumber and anchoring these crude floats—each tied to a length of rope weighted by a stone—along the stretch of water ahead of the boat. She then churned triumphantly over them to shore—"eating up the lights," as the procedure was called—while fascinated passengers peered into the gloom from the bow.

A pilot tied up as storms approached, too—if he had time—because the flat bottoms and high superstructures of steamboats left them almost incapable of maneuvering when they were caught in open water by one of those boiling valley thunderstorms that, in the words of an Army officer who regularly traveled the Missouri, "caused the river to yield up clouds of spray like the vortex of Niagara."

A pilot had, eternally, to "read water"—to guess at a glance the speed of a current in a bend, and to decide from surface swirls and ripples whether the river concealed rocks, sand bars or snags. Nature intruded as he did so. Wind sometimes helped him, tending to ruffle deep water dramatically. But rain dappled the whole surface and laid a blur of tiny splashes over the river's mysteries. Surface glare masked them, too, when the sun lay lower than 45 degrees above the horizon; and so also, during windy days at low water, did drifting sand from the river's dunelike bars. It took courage and skill to accept such minimal indications as remained and keep a boat moving.

Roustabouts punched a long pole to the bottom, rather than heaving a lead-weighted line, when a pilot began tapping his bell for soundings on the shallow Missouri—and they chanted the depth, while stabbing away, at every contact with the bottom. But good pilots depended on the "feel" of the steamboat as well. A vessel behaved differently as the water grew shallower, or as the speed of the current began to increase. This sense of the vessel's own reaction to the river was crucial; the pilot had only split seconds for decisions that kept the craft whole.

Still, the steamer—like the cowboy's mean and hard-mouthed mount—was exactly what it had to be: cheap enough to float cargo and make money; powerful enough to master a current that, in places, ran 10 miles per hour or even faster; and simple enough to be operated and repaired by uneducated engine-room crews.

The steamboat did not assume its role as the dominant mode of transportation on the Missouri without incessant criticism as well as incessant difficulty. Explosions and snaggings prompted torrents of remonstrance from press and pulpit; and the less-than-luxurious accommodations and the rudeness of propulsive equipment provoked endless complaint from writers, engineers and travelers from abroad. But the operators of the paddle wheelers—as well as the vast majority of passengers who risked their necks on them—responded to steam power with an astonishing optimism.

None maintained a cheerier view than a young inventor-engineer named Nicholas Roosevelt (Teddy's great granduncle), who took the first of all Western steamers from Pittsburgh to New Orleans in 1811—simply to show that it could be done—and by his example opened the whole trans-Mississippi wilderness to paddle navigation. Roosevelt's vessel, built at Pittsburgh by Robert Livingston and Robert Fulton and named, with forthright optimism, *New Orleans,* was wonderfully unsuited to its role: underpowered, deep-hulled like an ocean-going ship, and slow to answer the helm. When the voyage was announced, local rivermen decided Roosevelt was some sort of homicidal maniac. He not only proposed to negotiate the Falls of the Ohio—a two-mile stretch where the Ohio River below Louisville dropped 22 feet over limestone ledges—but to take along his pregnant wife Lydia while thus killing himself. Roosevelt simply smiled and persuaded a large crew to share the boat's fate: a captain, an engineer, a pilot, six deck hands (who were instructed to say, "Aye, aye, sir," when he addressed them), a waiter, a cook, two female servants—and his brother-in-law, who later wrote an account of the adventure.

An enormous Newfoundland dog named Tiger was led aboard on sailing day in late September, and barked in "jolly fashion" at crowds that ran to the riverbank as

The anatomy of a Missouri River stern-wheeler

Smaller, slower and far less glamorous than the floating palaces that plied the Mississippi, the Missouri River stern-wheeler nonetheless was a triumph of shallow-water design. Its draft was so slight that one humorist described the vessel as being "so built that when the river is low and the sand bars come out for air, the first mate can tap a keg of beer and run four miles on the suds."

From its spoonlike bow, shaped for sliding over shoals, to its huge paddle wheel that dipped only a few inches into the water, the Missouri boat was built for muddy going. A typical upper-Missouri "mountain boat" like the celebrated *Far West,* illustrated below and shown in cutaway views on the following pages, could carry 200 tons of freight and up to 30 cabin pas-

sengers through waist-high water. Unloaded, she could proceed safely with as little as 20 inches of river under her flat bottom.

Such remarkable performance was achieved by an ingenious construction that stacked 80 per cent of the bulk above the water line, giving the boat its distinctive wedding-cake silhouette. Directly above the broad, low hull — virtually awash when fully loaded — was the open-sided main deck that housed fireboxes, engines, firewood, cargo and low-paying deck passengers. Covering the main deck was the boiler deck,

where more affluent travelers were assigned small private compartments in an enclosed cabin, topped in turn by an open hurricane deck for promenading.

Some boats rose even higher out of the water than the *Far West* with yet another abbreviated deck, where the boat's officers were quartered. But always at the peak was the boxy wheelhouse, windowed on all four sides to give the pilot a 360-degree view of the hazard-filled river.

As a last defense against sand bars that could not be steered around, slid over or smashed through by the intrepid pilot, every Missouri stern-wheeler boasted a pair of "grasshoppers" — sturdy wooden spars that could be lowered into the mud and used like giant crutches to "walk the boat" to deeper water.

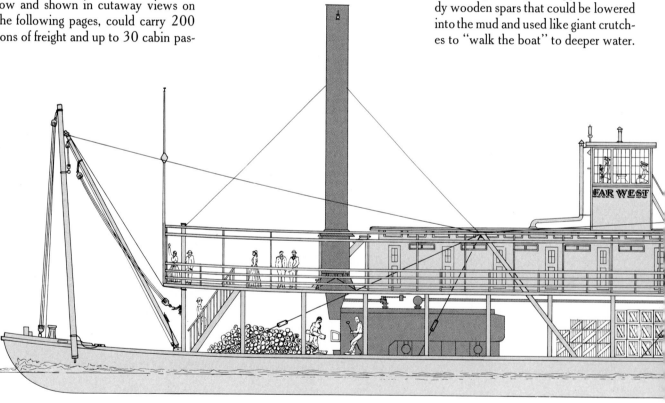

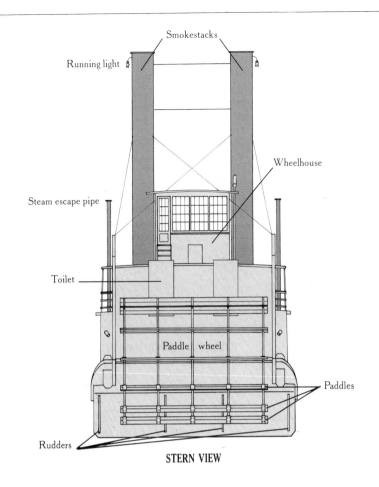

Smokestacks

Running light

Wheelhouse

Steam escape pipe

Toilet

Paddle wheel

Paddles

Rudders

STERN VIEW

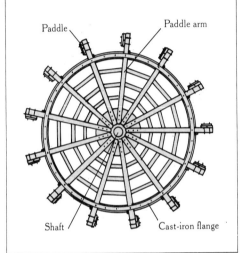

260 DIPS A MINUTE

Far West's paddle wheel, seen below and in the stern view at left, was a simply constructed wooden cylinder 18 feet in diameter and 24 feet wide and belted with cast iron. Two engines rotated the wheel about 20 times — or 260 paddle dips — per minute, providing the thrust to overcome currents that could exceed 10 miles per hour.

Paddle

Paddle arm

Shaft

Cast-iron flange

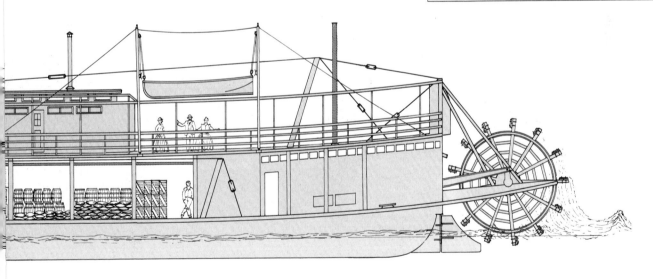

0   5   10   15   20 feet

An 1844 flier announces that part ownership of the steamer *Ione* is up for sale. The winning bidder received a harsh lesson in the chanciness of steamboating on the Missouri: his investment sank in two years.

ADMINISTRATOR'S SALE.

I WILL SELL TO THE HIGHEST BIDDER, FOR CASH, THE

 One-eighth part   of the Steamboat

IONE,

On THURSDAY, the 28th inst., at 10 A.M.,

OF THAT DAY,

In front of the Store of Messrs. McCalister & Co.,

ON WATER STREET,

Being the interest in said boat belonging to the Estate of Matthew Hogan, deceased.

SAINT LOUIS, March 6, 1844.   **M. BLAIR, Administrator.**

the boat went hissing and clanking downstream. Roosevelt and his craft moved from one triumph to another. His wife retired to her cabin after the boat was moored at Louisville and proceeded to give birth to a son. Boat, crew, dog and infant then rushed unscathed through the falls with five inches of draft to spare. They weathered an earthquake that shattered towns in the Mississippi Valley, produced severe flooding and — according to the journey's chronicler — caused general seasickness aboard the boat. They inspired "shouts of exaltation" at Natchez, and were received as symbols of the glorious future when they anchored, after three months of intermittent steaming, at New Orleans on January 12, 1812.

Steamboats began proliferating, almost instantaneously, upon the Western rivers. The early versions were fully as unsuitable for these shallow waters as *New Orleans* had been, and they had to combat nature without recourse to Roosevelt's luck — or the luxury of always heading downstream. These handicaps did not prevent them from being launched on unlikely adventures. Only seven years after Roosevelt's feat, Secretary of War John C. Calhoun decided to send a fleet of steamboats 2,000 miles up the Missouri to the mouth of the Yellowstone, where a fort would be erected to deter British incursions into American territory. An Ohio River steamboat operator, James Johnson, received a lucrative contract to supply five vessels—plus crews—for the mission. Congress ordered the construction of a sixth, *Western Engineer,* with upper works built to resemble a scaly serpent that would emit steam through its nostrils and thus frighten off any Indians who might be inclined to hostility.

The fleet headed up the Missouri on June 21, 1819 — an ill-chosen starting date, since the river's spring rise had passed. Johnson's boats, designed for deeper waters, failed to make it past the Kansas River, 400 miles upstream. *Western Engineer* ran aground twice in two miles after entering the Missouri and managed to get only as far as the present site of Omaha — 1,135 miles from her destination. Congress took a bitter view of this performance, and when a second expedition to the Yellowstone River was authorized five years later the legislators specified transportation that did not rely on the steam engine.

Legend credits an ex-keelboater named Henry M. Shreve (for whom Shreveport, Louisiana, is named) with creating the powerful, light-draft, multidecked successors to these early paddle boats and with doing so in one fell swoop when he built an improved steamer named *Washington* at Wheeling, West Virginia, in 1816. Shreve put the boat's boiler (though not her engine) up on deck, thus anticipating the idea — soon universally adopted — of taking the whole power plant out of the increasingly shallow hold and installing it on top of the hull. But *Washington* was little different, in other respects, from her sisters of the period.

Western steamers, in fact, were developed over a period of many decades, and vessels used in upper-Missouri travel were still being refined well into the 1870s. The upper-river boat, in its final form, was broad and flat-bottomed for light draft and possessed a spoon-shaped bow for climbing sand bars. It also had accumulated the wedding-cake superstructure — main deck, boiler deck, hurricane deck, officers' quarters and pilothouse — that made its appearance unique; this high superstructure eliminated the need for a deep hold by the upward distribution of passenger and cargo spaces.

Almost all such changes sprang from a kind of workman's practicality rather than from exercises in theory. Most boat and engine builders were refugees from simpler trades: they had been carpenters, flatboat builders, makers of water wheels, blacksmiths, tinsmiths and begetters of backwoods stills. They worked by "cut and try," and "rule of thumb" — under the steady prodding of captains and owners who regularly visited shipyards to express their ideas on the proper design of Missouri

River craft. A philosophy of recklessness — wafted east from the frontier — was a continuous ingredient in the process of evolution. Missouri rivermen showed little inclination to reduce the risks of their trade if it meant paying higher prices for the boats. In 1839, when shipyards experimented with iron hulls — which were far less vulnerable to snags than wooden ones, but twice as expensive — they found no takers among the men who plied the most snag-infested river of all.

It was the rare riverman who did not delight in gimcrackery to add an air of grandeur to his calling. Most vessels bore friezes of wooden scrollwork around cabins and pilothouse; and captains ordered sunbursts, leaping deer or other suggestive heraldry painted in primary colors on their paddle boxes. Whistles did not come into general use until the 1850's — boats signaled with bells alone before this, or sometimes "vented steam" as a salute when meeting another vessel. But, once adopted, whistles lent steamboating its ultimate touch of drama and romance, particularly after manufacturers produced three-toned and five-toned models that played chords and could raise echoes along miles of winding river valley. Sweetness of tone was prized in both signaling devices: Captain John C. Elliott melted 500 silver dollars into the metal from which the bell for his steamer *Emma C. Elliott* was cast, hoping to get a superior sound.

Peripatetic author Robert Forbes refused to be cozened by such theatrics: "The habitual traveler by water," he warned readers in a magazine article, "should carry a bag of vulcanized rubber with means for inflation by mouth, and with 'beckets' or handles to use it as a float." Editors of the *North American Review* seemed resigned, however, to the travelers' preference for swiftness over safety: "It is vain to supply life preservers as a means of inducement to passengers if another steamboat, lying alongside, has proved faster in a trial of speed."

Speed and power to achieve it: these were the fundamental goals of the steamboatman. No single aspect of the paddle vessel's development inspired such an amalgam of rashness and ingenuity, was attended by such a blend of ignorance and intuition, or yielded such flawed but dazzling results as did the struggle to create engines and boilers worthy of the Western rivers. Pittsburgh's mechanics and ironworkers had to puzzle out new methods of working metal as well as new ways of

A flotilla of stern- and side-wheelers lines a boatyard on the Monongahela at Brownsville, Pennsylvania. Though 1,200 miles from the Missouri, Brownsville was the hub of Western riverboat construction in the 1870s, chiefly because the heavy industry for engine-building was in nearby Pittsburgh.

103

using it, and they had to cope with a mysterious and dangerous new force while doing so.

The direction of their efforts was set by Oliver Evans, a Delaware farmer's son who combined mechanical skill with an imaginative mind and who vastly influenced industrial innovation in the infant United States. Evans engaged in pre-Revolutionary War experiments with steam when he was only 17, invented (but did not develop) a self-propelled carriage, and built scores of engines for factories and steamboats before he died in 1819.

Early American vessels were powered by copies of the Boulton and Watts engine that Robert Fulton imported from England in 1807. These devices used very low pressures, and they condensed steam as it left the cylinder to create a vacuum and thereby induce atmospheric force to help move the piston. They were complicated, unresponsive, excessively big and heavy, and—because they stood upright and their pistons moved straight up and down—they pounded like pile drivers on the framework of hulls. Evans—or rather his ideas—caused these old engines to become outmoded within a very few years and granted the Western steamboat that hazardous practicality that permitted it to perform as an instrument of American destiny in the half century ahead.

Evans had already proved that a light, cheap, simple factory engine with a small piston could exhaust directly into the air and still produce far more power than cumbersome condensing engines if it was fed steam at high pressure. Indeed, it could double or triple this power output if one dared keep the pressure rising through "hard firing" of the boiler. Such engines weighed only five tons, as compared to 100 tons for less powerful low-pressure models, and Evans set out to apply them to boats. But he also incautiously described his ideas in a book entitled (apparently because he was overthrowing previous guidelines to the usage of steam): *The Abortion of the Young Steam Engineer's Guide: Containing an Investigation of the Principles, Construction and Powers of Steam Engines.*

Other mechanics—chief among them Daniel French of Brownsville, Pennsylvania, and Thomas Copeland of Pittsburgh—ignored his patent and began developing high-pressure engines themselves. "They use your strong steam," Evans' son, George, wrote to him in 1814, "and say you dare not molest them." This turned out to be the fact, and the Evans engine—wrenched, no matter how dubiously, into the public domain—was utilized in almost all Western steamers from the 1820s on. It provided the kind of propulsion necessary to cope with fast water, and it made light-draft hulls possible: builders distributed its weight and eliminated pounding by installing the single cylinder on its side and by then connecting the piston rod to the paddle-wheel crank with an iron-bound pine log known as the "pitman."

Steam was generated for paddle-boat engines by batteries of two, four or more long, cylindrical wrought-iron boilers. They were mounted fore and aft and in parallel, and were perforated lengthwise by two or three pipelike flues through which hot gases from the fires were led to increase heating efficiency. Their fireboxes opened toward the bow end of the boat—to utilize the breeze created by forward motion—and were surmounted by a pair of iron chimneys (never called stacks or funnels) that rose up through the vessel's superstructure and towered as much as 100 feet above her upper deck. These steamboat boilers were prodigious sources of energy, but for many decades they visited harrowing risks and hardships upon passengers and crew.

All Western vessels used river water to make steam, and since a cubic foot of brown liquid from the Missouri could contain handfuls of silt and sand, steamboats usually ended a day's run on the Big Muddy by extinguishing the fires, draining and opening the boilers, and sending a hapless fireman inside to shovel them free of steaming mud. The muck caused trouble even after boilermakers devised ways of blowing it out under pressure while a boat was underway, for it still worked its way back into the engines to grind away at valves and pistons. But engine-room crews had concerns more disturbing than this.

Water and pressure gauges did not come into general use until the middle 1850s, and engine crews had to rely mostly on instinct in detecting when boilers were running dry or building steam to dangerous levels. No early engineers really understood—and neither did many of the best technical minds of the day—how fast steam pressures rose as firing was increased. There were experts, in fact, who believed explosions were caused by a mysterious "boiler gas" and not by steam at all. Multiple boilers became doubly dangerous when a boat developed a list; they were connected by pipes calculated to equalize the level of liquid in all of them, but water invariably drained away from the one that was tilted highest by wind or improper loading. Flues turned red hot and collapsed in minutes when thus deprived of internal cooling, cooking everyone within range in a roaring burst of superheated steam.

Not all of the risks originated in the machinery. "The management of engines and boilers is entrusted," wrote visiting English engineer David Stevenson in 1838, "to men whose carelessness of human life is equalled only by their want of civilization." A few years later, one pleader for Congressional reform complained of "filthy engine rooms" being "placed under the charge of mere boys in intellect, in whom enormous wages produce profligacy and recklessness." The more famous mountain pilots could attract steady and knowledgeable engineers, but many captains forgave drunkenness and ignorance in a man who could get his vessel away from landings like lightning, thereby impressing bystanders, and who had some skill as a blacksmith. The Missouri boat that suffered a mechanical breakdown in the wilderness might molder there forever if her engineer could not "pound iron" and make temporary repairs.

An engineer's bargain with the owners was a simple one. They paid him about $200 a month, provided him with an anvil and a forge, applauded him for dealing with dangerous levels of steam pressure, and were always ready to commend him for bravery if he blew himself up, or to deplore him publicly for any accident he might survive.

The competence of engine-room crews rose, in time, and the most horrendous failings of mechanical equipment were gradually eliminated—particularly after Congress voted for federal inspection of steamboats in 1838. But boiler pressures rose, too. Engines used steam at 150 or 160 pounds to the square inch by mid-century—a far cry from the 40 pounds originally prescribed by Oliver Evans. And the boldest engineers overweighted safety valves to push pressures higher when boats approached a stretch of fast water. There was nothing like a "wad of steam"—as rivermen put it—to get a vessel out of trouble in rapids. And there was no way to store this energy for such extraordinary demands save by the ticklish business of bottling up

steam and hoping to release it through the engines in time to avoid disaster.

The lower Missouri was dominated for many years by that classic Western steamboat, the double-engined side-wheeler—prized for the maneuverability it would grant a pilot if one paddle wheel was reversed while the other maintained forward motion. Mountain boats were almost exclusively stern-wheelers. This arrangement saved weight, protected the paddle from snags and permitted a broader-beam hull—hence lighter draft and more cargo capacity. Moreover, stern-wheelers were useful in shallows because their paddles would raise the level of water under the hull if run in reverse while the boat was being grasshoppered over a bar.

Side-wheelers required two engineers at all times—and demanded a high degree of teamwork from them in tricky water. But men at the engine throttles of all boats needed concentration and physical strength when negotiating—as one engine-room veteran put it—"a piece of crooked river with the boat dodging about among reefs and bars and the bells coming faster than you could answer them." There were times when the most conscientious of engineers became so involved that they could not have rectified—or very probably even sensed—an overproduction of steam that was going to kill them in 30 seconds.

A certain fatalism seems to have become ingrained in steamboat crews by the exigencies of their trade. Boatyards found it increasingly difficult, as hulls grew shallower, to achieve rigidity by internal bracing. Most boats were so limber that engines were thrown in and out of line on turns, and steam lines were constantly subject to hissing leaks. The boats had other peculiarities that crews had to anticipate. The paddle of a stern-wheeler would slow down from 24 to as few as 14 revolutions a minute when she got into shallow water, because the paddle could not easily pull water through the narrow gap between the hull and the bottom. Side-wheelers, passing a sand bar to port or starboard, veered toward the shallows, because the paddle on the deep-water side had more pulling power.

It was hard to guess which way to jump—if a prospective victim had opportunity to guess at all—when things went wrong on a Missouri steamer. One fireman drowned when he leaped into the river after a boiler's

A side-wheeler slips cautiously through a cluster of snags — sunken trees that often weighed tons — in this panorama by Karl Bodmer. Many snag

were below the surface, and though pilots were always alert for warning swirls, these obstructions caused almost two thirds of all steamer wrecks.

An 1838 patent diagram reveals the work-
ings of a "snag boat," a double-hull vessel
devised by shipbuilder Henry Shreve. It ran
directly at sunken trees, scooped them up
and hauled them aboard with a windlass.

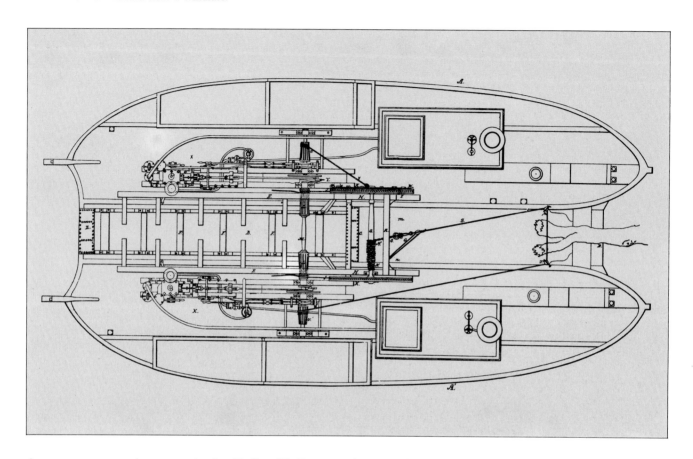

dome gave way on the stern-wheeler *Belle of Jefferson*
in 1874. The steam blew harmlessly upward and
spared his mates who stayed aboard. Fifty-five German
immigrants were scalded to death, however, when boiler flues of the side-wheeler *Edna* collapsed from over-
heating at Green Island in 1842.

Fate seemed infinitely fickle on the Missouri. The
steamboat *Big Hatchie* killed 35 people and wounded
many more when she blew up near Hermann, Missouri,
in 1845. But most of the side-wheeler *Timour*'s passengers escaped a boiler explosion that killed captain,
pilot and clerk while she was taking on wood near Jefferson City in August 1854; they were picking wild-
flowers on a bluff above the river when she went up,
and escaped injury even when the boat's safe landed
among them like a gigantic cannon ball. Passengers and
crew of the mountain boat *Chippewa* got ashore to a
man when she caught fire near Montana's Poplar River
in 1861, and they watched in complete safety — having
cast her adrift — when her cargo of gunpowder blew her
into a cloud of splinters and caused one of the biggest

bangs in Western history. The crew members of the
mountain boat *Kate Sweeney* also made it to shore
without incident when she went down near the Ver-
milion River in August 1855, but were slaughtered by
Indians when they set off downstream on foot.

High winds sometimes wrecked steamboats with no
more warning than a boiler explosion. In one such case,
the mountain boat *Osceola* was making her way up the
Yellowstone River in the summer of 1877 when some
cowboys aboard spotted a white stallion in a herd of
wild horses on shore. The captain obligingly halted the
steamer and waited for two hours while the cowboys
roped the stallion, hauled it back to the boat, and tied it
to a stanchion. The boat was demolished moments later by a tornado — from which hills up ahead might have
shielded her had she not loitered so rashly at the bank.
All of the humans survived, but the white stallion, as
was noted with satisfaction by the crew, went down
with the hull.

Drifting ice was also a menace, although every captain did his best to get back downstream by late au-

tumn and owners usually delayed upstream voyages until the worst of the river's winter burden had washed away. Still, ice could do terrible damage even in downriver ports. An entire fleet of steamboats was ground to kindling wood at St. Louis during "The Great Ice Gorge of 1856." Rising water broke the solid, heavy ice near the city in late February, piled huge sections of it into vast, noisy hills and ridges and moved these grinding masses slowly downstream with every movable object they encountered. Dozens of boats were torn from their moorings at the St. Louis levee, then solid with steamers for 20 blocks.

"The ice at first moved slowly," reported *The Missouri Republican,* "and without perceptible shock. But the steamers *Australia, Adriatic, Brunette, Paul Jones, Falls City, Altoona, A.B. Chambers* and *Challenge* all were torn away from the shore and floated down with the immense fields of ice. The first obstacles with which they came in contact were a large fleet of barges and canal boats, about fifty in all, which were either sunk, broken or carried away. *Bon Accord* and *High-*

land Mary were carried off . . . both total losses . . . and after them *Lamartine, Westerner* and *Jeanie Deans. Gossamer, Luella, Alice* and *Badger State* were forced ashore only slightly damaged . . . but *Shenandoah* was wrecked, *G.W. Sparhawk* sunk and *Clara* and *Ben Bolt* were badly damaged.

"The character of the ice changed after running about one hour and came down in frothy, crumbled condition. Just before the river gorged, huge piles of ice twenty and thirty feet in height were forced up by the current at the Lower Dyke where so many boats had come to a halt. These boats seemed to be literally buried in ice. At six o'clock P.M. the river had risen at least ten feet. The current was now much more swift and the night very dark, a heavy and steady rain having set in. The terrible sweep of waters with its burden of ice, the mashing to pieces of boats and the hurrying on shore of the excited crowd was one of the most awful and imposing scenes we have ever witnessed."

Grant Marsh, later to become one of the most famous upper-river pilots, was the winter watchman on

An extract from a report by Captain Hiram Chittenden of the Army Corps of Engineers spells out the circumstances surrounding some of the 295 steamboat disasters on the Missouri between 1819 and 1897.

List of steamboat wrecks on the Missouri River, from the beginning of steamboat navigation to the present time

Name of boat.	Description of boat.	Trade engaged in, and owners and officers.	Date of wreck.	Locality of wreck.	Cause of wreck.	Remarks.
Dacotah (No. 2)....	Stern-wheel; about 250 by 40 feet; 956 tons.	St. Louis and Kansas City..	Sept. 17, 1884	Near Providence, Mo...	Snag...	Was raised, towed to New Orleans, and dismantled. Her machinery is now on the steamer Imperial, in the New Orleans-Red River trade.
Dallas	Stern-wheel; small boat.	Missouri River trade........	Sometime in the seventies.	Morgans Island........	....do	
Damsel	Stern-wheel ..	Circus boat. Charles Davis, pilot.	1876	Head of Onawa Bend.	....do	Had on board a circus company. Capt. Joseph La Barge came along on the John M. Chambers and took off the passengers.
Dan Converse.....	....do	Missouri River trade........	Nov. 15, 1858	10 miles above St. Joseph, Mo.	....do	An old boat, valued at $3,000. Boat and cargo a total loss. No lives lost.
Daniel G. Taylor...	Side-wheel; about 240 by 38 feet; 543 tons.	Mountain trade	July 5, 1856	3 miles below Rocheport; head of Paynes Island.	....do	Was afterwards raised and worn out on the Lower Mississippi. She was a peculiar looking boat, having side wheels, but clear back at the stern. Named for a mayor of St. Louis, Mo.
Dart...............	Side-wheel; single engine.	Missouri River trade. Partially owned and commanded by Capt. John Cleveland.	1838	1 mile below Glasgow, Mo.	Rocks	
Dells	Stern-wheel ..	Missouri River trade........	Oct. 26, 1878	Above Arago, Nebr...	Snag and explosion.	Struck snag and exploded her boilers and sank. Boat and cargo a total loss. No insurance. 2 lives lost.
Dew Drop..........	Stern-wheel; 148 tons.	....do	June, 1860	Mouth of Osage River.	Fire	
Delaware..........	Side-wheel....	....do	1857	Smiths Bar, Missouri.	Snag........	
Denver (No. 1).....	Side-wheel; 225 by 33 feet; 300 tons.	St. Joseph and Omaha. Owned by the Hannibal and St. Joseph R. R. Co. John Waddell, master.	May 16, 1867	St. Joseph, Mo.	Fire	Named for the first governor of Colorado. The wreck was afterwards rebuilt into the Denver No. 2. The Denver No. 1 burnt while lying at the wharf at St. Joseph, Mo.
Denver (No. 2).....	Center-wheel..	St. Joseph and Omaha, and ferrying.	Mar. 13, 1880	Opposite Fort Lincoln, N. Dak.	Ice........	Built out of the wreck of the Denver No. 1.
Diana.............	Side-wheel....	Missouri River trade. Owned by the American Fur Co. Capt. John Shallcross, master.	Oct., 1836	Diana Bend. 2½ miles above Rocheport, Mo.	Snag........	Built for the Cincinnati and Louisville Packet Company by Capt. Joe Swagers, one of the founders of above line. The steamer Diana was wrecked twice; the first time March, 1836, when she was bound for Council Bluffs, by striking a snag near Lexington. Her cargo was put ashore, but high water carried most of it off. The boat was temporarily repaired, brought to St. Louis and fixed up. She was next wrecked by striking a snag 2½ miles above Rocheport, in what is now known as Diana Bend. Part of the cargo was saved. There was some expectation that the boat would be raised, but she was abandoned.
Don Cameron, J....	Stern-wheel ..	Government transport......	May 17, 1877	Omaha and Winnebago Agency.	....do	This boat was built by the United States Government for the Yellowstone River. She was transporting baggage and private property for the Fifth Infantry, from Fort Leavenworth to Fort Keogh, on the Yellowstone River, and sank on her first trip. No Missouri River pilot was on the boat. The boat was being steered by an officer. Boat and cargo a total loss. Several lawsuits grew out of this disaster. No lives lost.
Dugan, R. W.....	Stern-wheel; 160 by 32 feet.	Missouri River trade. Capt. Joe Kinney, sr., owner. Capt. Joe Kenney, jr., master.	Oct. 21, 1878	2 miles below Dewitt, Mo.	....do	Boat and cargo total loss. No lives lost.
Duncan Carter.....	Side-wheel; 221 by 33 feet.	Missouri River trade........	Aug. 28, 1858	Augusta Bend..........	....do	Sank on down trip from Weston to St. Louis, in 12 feet of water. Boat and cargo a total loss. She was 2 years old and was valued at $44,000.
Durfee, E. H.......	Stern-wheel; 175 by 36 feet.	St. Louis and Kansas City..	May 23, 1881	Mouth of Gasconade River.	Overloaded .	This boat was named for one of the members of the firm of Durfee & Peck, fur traders. She was on a down trip and was fully loaded, but, on arrival at Portland, 8 miles above the Gasconade, she took on a large amount of wheat. She commenced sinking soon after swinging into the stream and went down at the mouth of the Gasconade River in deep water. Boat and cargo a total loss. Boat was valued at $18,000. No lives lost.
Durock	Side-wheel....	Missouri River trade; John McCloy, master.	1852	St. Charles Bend.......	Snag........	
Eagle	Stern-wheel; 125 by 25 feet.	Ferryboat	Feb. 27, 1897	Lexington, Mo.........	Burnt	A gasoline stove exploded and set boat on fire. Boat was a total loss. Wreck removed by U. S. snag boat C. R. Suter, June 16, 1897.
Eaton, N. J........	Side-wheel....	Glasgow packet.............	Apr. 9, 1856	Augusta Bend..........	Snag........	Wrecked on her first trip up the Missouri River. Boat a total loss. She was valued at $38,000. The deck load was saved, balance of cargo was lost.
Eclipse	Stern-wheel; 178 by 31 feet.	Fort Benton trade. I. G. Baker, owner.	Sept. 3, 1887	15 miles below Sioux City, Iowa.	....do	Boat and cargo a total loss. No lives lost.
Edgar	Stern-wheel....	Missouri River trade........	Mar. 26, 1884	Near Omaha, Nebr....	Ice.........	Boat valued at $3,500; insured at $2,000.
Edna	Side-wheel....	Glasgow packet.............	July 3, 1842	Green Island at the mouth of the Missouri River.	Boiler explosion.	Named for one of Captain McCord's daughters. The flues collapsed in both boilers and killed about 55 German emigrants.
Ella Kimbrough...	Stern-wheel; 243 tons.	Missouri River trade. Capt. T. N. Kimbrough.	Sept. 20, 1884	St. Charles Chute.....	Snag........	This boat was formerly the General Sherman, a United States steamer. She was bought from the Government by P. P. Manion, who sold her to Captain Kimbrough, who named her for his wife. When wrecked she had on board 3,000 sacks of wheat. Boat and cargo a total loss; cargo was insured for $8,000. No lives lost.
Elk................	Side-wheel, small steamer, single engine.	Missouri River trade........	1838	Massie's wood yard, 5 miles below Hermann, Mo.	....do	Passengers taken off by Capt. Joseph La Barge on the steamer Kansas.
El Paso............	Side-wheel; about 180 by 28 feet; about 267 tons.	Missouri River trade. Capt. Bill Terrell, owner; Capt. W. R. Massie, master.	Apr. 10, 1855	Foot of Franklins Island, just below Booneville at Whites Landing.	Snag........	Boat and cargo a total loss. No lives lost.

A.B. Chambers that day, and he stayed aboard as ice swept her away. Both he and his ship were lucky; *A. B. Chambers* was borne gradually back toward shore during the night and came to rest, still afloat, three miles from her original mooring place.

Marsh had yet another glimpse of the forces inherent in river ice, and survived an even closer brush with death, during the winter of 1859. Both he and a young riverman named Samuel Clemens were serving aboard a boat called (by curious coincidence) *A.B. Chambers No. 2* when she ran aground near Commerce, Missouri. Marsh was the mate and Clemens, soon to take the pen name of Mark Twain, was second pilot. The vessel burned up her wood supply while vainly attempting to extricate herself, and Marsh set off in her yawl with a crew of husky oarsmen — and with Clemens acting as steersman — to order a barge load of fresh fuel from a woodyard on shore.

The river's main channel was clogged with moving floes, but Clemens directed the yawl around them to the shore opposite the woodyard, crept cautiously past an island, and eventually — below an ice jam where drifting cakes were fast collecting — found clear water leading across the stream to her destination. But the ice jam rumbled and broke as the boat entered the space below it, and Marsh found himself yelling, "Turn back quick, Sam! Back!" Clemens looked over his shoulder and said almost conversationally, "No. Go ahead as fast as you can." He was right. Acres of grinding ice closed up behind the yawl and her wildly laboring oarsmen, but patches of water opened ahead and she narrowly scraped through to safety.

But ice, no matter how dangerous, was not nearly so much a source of peril as were snags, rocks and shoals. Missouri steamboats spitted themselves by the score, year after year, on these obstructions and seemed to do so, at times, out of some perversity of their own. In 1867 the side-wheeler *New Sam Gaty* — for reasons that were never determined — suddenly veered out of control near Arrow Rock, Missouri, smashed into an obstruction, listed wildly, caught fire and burned up, all in the space of one hectic hour.

Reminders of the steamboat's fallibility were visible everywhere. Cora Island was created in 1869 when the side-wheeler *Cora Number 3* struck a snag and sank near Bellefontaine Bluffs, Missouri, altering the hydraulics of the river and attracting rising layers of mud and sand that eventually supported grasses, bushes and trees. The river simply moved away from other disabled boats. When the stern-wheeler *James H. Trover* suffered a broken boiler pump and was caught immobile against the bank in eastern Montana Territory in 1867, the stream abruptly altered its course, leaving her high and dry forever.

But if the steamboat was subject to constant tribulation on the Missouri, it was often able to survive the worst the river had to offer. For decades boats multiplied faster than they went down. In 1859 alone more than 100 vessels plied the river regularly, splashing over the bones of their predecessors in bend after bend. The steamboat's record of accomplishment, all things considered, was astonishing; and in the final analysis the catalogue of its mishaps is significant only as a measure of the odds surmounted and the prices paid by the men who created for it such a strategic role in Western history.

The steamer was indeed served, in many cases, "by men of coarse habit, recklessness, and uneducated mind," as an 1838 government report declared. But critics forgot, while complaining, that men like these were exactly the sort who braved the Blackfeet to trap beaver, and who thronged mining camps, roped and punched cattle and crossed the mountains to California and Oregon. It is quite possible that fewer steamboats would have exploded had they been in the hands of engineers with more training or wisdom, and it is certain that fewer would have gone up in flames had they been manned by teetotalers, since crewmen, in the hope of stealing whiskey, were known to light their way into steamer holds with candles.

Yet it seems doubtful that the paddle vessel could have so routinely exceeded its own potentialities in the West — or have exerted the influence it did — had it been in the hands of more prudent men. Boat builders did not really expect their steamers — even those designed for the upper Missouri — to cope with the swift, rock-strewn Yellowstone; and they certainly did not believe their deep-hulled, heavy lower-river boats could survive the Missouri's 198-mile stretch of shallow rapids and rock reefs between Cow Island and Fort Benton. But captains damned the risk and took them there anyhow — and, if a boat survived, took it back another time.

Casualties of a cantankerous river

If a flimsy Western steamer ever ventured out to sea, mused a 19th Century wit, "the ocean would take one playful slap at it and people would be picking up kindling on the beach for the next eleven years." Even on the Missouri River, steamboats were victimized by a whole catalogue of calamities: they were consumed by fire, crushed by ice, impaled by snags, torn apart by high winds, blown to smithereens by devastating boiler explosions, and occasionally brought to an ignominious end in collisions with sturdy railroad bridges.

Many wrecks, however, were not the catastrophes one might imagine. Passengers and crewmen learned to flee to the high, open hurricane deck when the alarm bell sounded, confident that even if the pilot could not quickly ground his stricken craft on the nearest bank or sand bar, the boat would probably not sink deep enough to wet their feet. The shallowness of the Missouri was also a salvager's boon; at least 20 of the steamers wrecked on the river were easily refloated.

Surely the hardiest of these resurrected vessels was the mountain boat *Benton*. She first came to grief when she hit a snag in 1889. Raised and repaired, she had an uneventful second life until 1895, when she again struck a snag and sank. Restored to service again, the *Benton* lasted another two years before a bridge collision reduced her to the hopeless hulk shown here.

Her chimneys askew and her back broken, *Benton* draws a curious crowd near Sioux City after her third wreck in 1897. While approaching a drawbridge, she ran into submerged pilings, careened out of control, slammed into the bridge and drifted to her final rest not far downriver.

Crushed against the St. Louis levee by ice floating down-river, steamers gradually crumble into ruin in a drawn-out disaster that continued through much of the winter of 1865-1866. Twenty-one steamboats were destroyed in all — six of them during a surge of ice that lasted only five minutes.

Beset by a savage storm at the Bismarck levee in 1879, the brand-new *Montana*—one of the largest stern-wheelers—had most of her superstructure torn off. Some pieces were discovered 500 yards away. She was repaired and sailed five more years before her second and fatal mishap *(over)*.

The luckless *Montana* rests on the bottom of the shallow river at St. Charles, Missouri, in 1884, after a capricious current forced her against the supports of the railroad bridge in the background. Although some of her cargo was saved, the boat—valued at $40,000—was declared a total loss.

Hung up on a sand bar, the steamer *Yellowstone* has her cargo lightened in order to refloat her in this 1833 scene by artist Karl Bodmer.

4 | No buoys, no beacons, no maps

Before a pilot could take a steamboat into the Missouri he was expected, in the words of a veteran riverman, to "know the river as a schoolboy knows a path to the schoolhouse, upside down, endways, inside, outside and crossways." But even with an encyclopedic knowledge of snags, sand bars and landmarks, earned during a period of grueling apprenticeship that might last as long as five years, a steamboat pilot could rarely let down his guard and relax on a river regarded as one of the world's most difficult to travel safely.

"Navigating the Missouri at low water," wrote one observer, "is like putting a steamer on dry land and sending a boy ahead with a sprinkling pot." Yet the hardy band of pilots attacked this task with great gusto. Without buoys, beacons or reliable maps to guide them along the ever-shifting channel, they steered deftly around freshly formed sand bars when they could — or ran smack across them full steam ahead if necessary. The inevitable groundings were shrugged off; any pilot worth his salt soon developed ingenious ways to free his boat.

By the 1850s the cockier pilots had even begun to run the lower river after dark, calculating their position by moonlight, by the echoes of their steam whistles and by familiar sounds ashore. It was a risky technique. One pilot, in the habit of steering to the sound of a dog yelping near a river-front cabin, ran hard aground one dark night when the dog decided to do its barking elsewhere.

The unsinkable wizards of the wheelhouse

Captain Joseph Marie La Barge—a handsome, muscular, vigorous man of French-Canadian lineage—was the most heralded mountain pilot of his day, and one of the two most famous steamboatmen ever to operate on the Missouri River. Few equaled him at working a steamer through unfamiliar channels; he possessed an intuitive sense of water and an uncommon feel for the vessel beneath his feet, and he embodied an amalgam of steadiness, daring and endurance that made him unique among his peers. And he had qualities beyond these. He had been a fur trader and understood Indians and their ways. La Barge was so confident of his ability to deal safely with them that, in 1847, he took his wife, Pelagie, to the upper river with him in the side-wheeler *Martha* (and, in so doing, showed her a corner of the West no white woman had seen before). But he found himself in trouble with Indians after he tied *Martha* up at Crow Creek in Dakota Territory.

Tribesmen of the Missouri valley were more intricately involved with white rivermen than legend suggests, particularly after steamboats began delivering government "annuities"—shipments of cloth, food and beads specified by treaty and intended to woo Indians away from their warring life style. Crow Creek's Yanktonai Sioux were not pleased when the government agent aboard *Martha* sent only part of their promised goods ashore and told them that the rest could be available at the American Fur Company post in Fort Pierre, 92 miles upstream. The Sioux were all too familiar with this form of frontier graft: fur companies bribed Indian agents to "store" annuities at their warehouses and then sold the goods to the same tribesmen to whom they had been consigned in the first place. Disgruntled Sioux now drifted toward the bank and stared blackly at the steamer—the most obvious symbol of white corruption at hand.

A high wind was blowing, its gusts whipping smoke from *Martha*'s chimneys and flattening the tall grasses ashore. La Barge decided, black looks or not, that it was safer to stay where he was than to pull out into the stream and risk the chance of being blown into shoal water. But he had 10 cords of wood piled on the bank—fuel he had originally intended to pick up on his return trip—and, having seen Indians react before to the kind of miserable little farce that had just been enacted, he decided to take the wood on board before one of the Sioux hit on the idea of setting it on fire.

In addition to its cargo of annuities, *Martha* was transporting a contingent of loud-talking mountain men toward the Rockies. La Barge sent for their commander, Etienne Provost—a renowned trapper, hunter, explorer and guide—and asked for help. Provost grinned and jerked his head at the Indians: "We are going to have some fun before we get that wood on board." Then he bawled, "Woodpile! Woodpile!" and waved his men ashore with *Martha*'s deck hands. The Sioux did not move until the gangplank was jammed with men; at that point they ran up with rawhide whips, which had been wrapped around their waists, and began flailing at the hapless whites—who threw their burdens in all directions and tumbled over one another in getting back on deck.

Provost bent double with laughter at his place beside La Barge on the boiler deck. "I told you," he yelled. "I told you!" He then went below, strolled down the plank and said, "Now, men, come back out here and get this wood." The wood gang returned to the bank and loaded up again. "Now go on board," said Provost. He turned

---

The wheelhouse, 40 feet above the water line, was the pilot's throne. Because of the river's unpredictability, he could rarely hold a course for more than 1,000 yards.

to the Indians. "Why don't you stop them? Are you afraid of *me*?" Not an Indian spoke. Not an Indian moved. The wood was rescued. The Sioux moved sullenly away.

La Barge watched them depart, left his windy station on deck, walked into the steamer's big passenger cabin, sat down to read and, in an hour, was caught off guard by an Indian attack for the first and only time in his long career on the river. The Sioux had been insulted beyond endurance; they fired a volley into the boat, killed one deck hand, rushed the gangplank unopposed, and—having learned something of steamboats in years of observing them on the river—seized buckets, opened the vessel's fire doors, and flooded the banks of embers under her boilers.

La Barge—returned to reality by gunfire, the tinkle of broken glass and the howls of the invaders—scrambled out the cabin's after door, ran to his wife's stateroom and dragooned a man into helping him pile mattresses against its door. When he burst back into the passenger cabin, the Sioux had begun crowding through its forward entryway with a fur company boss named Colin Campbell. "They want the boat," said Campbell. "They say they'll let the crew go if they get it. If not, they're going to kill everybody."

La Barge was struck by the fact that the Indians, having pushed into the unfamiliar cabin, made no move to advance farther. How long would their doubts and suspicions keep them huddled where they were? The undercarriage of *Martha*'s brass cannon had been damaged and the weapon was—alas—in the engine room awaiting repair. But La Barge nevertheless decided to try to bring it into play. He held up a reassuring hand, walked slowly out of the cabin, leaped down to the engine spaces, yelled for engineer Nathan Grismore—a "brave and noble fellow" he later said—and began stuffing powder into the gun. Grismore shoved in a double handful of boiler rivets. The two men rigged a pulley, swayed the weapon up to the next deck, and maneuvered it into the cabin's after end. La Barge lighted a cigar, puffed on it, lowered it toward the cannon, looked up at Camp-

bell and said, "Tell them that if they don't get off the boat I'll blow them all to hell!"

The gesture was enough. The horrified Indians fought one another to escape and, though La Barge and Grismore pushed the gun out on deck behind them, the intruders were in full flight and the incident was over by the time the two steamboatmen swung it into position to command the shore.

Or almost over. "I looked for my crew," La Barge remembered after the voyage, "I looked for the brave mountaineers. Where had they hidden, leaving the boat defenseless? They were hanging thick as sardines all over the paddles. I was so disgusted that I was disposed to set the wheels in motion and give them all a ducking, but the Indians had put out the fires and we had no steam."

La Barge indeed possessed the power to chastise his passengers as he wished; like many of his peers, he filled two roles, serving both as *Martha*'s captain—the highest legal authority on board and the overseer of all administrative matters—and also as her pilot, or helmsman. Hundreds of captain-pilots contended with the Missouri during the long day of paddle navigation on Western waters. Theirs was a contest that demanded moral stature, courage and a kind of stage presence as well as knowledge of water and wilderness. Two men emerged as archetypes of the breed: La Barge, who was the most acclaimed of rivermen during the era of the Rocky Mountain fur trade, and Grant Marsh, the greatest of the steamboatmen drawn up the Missouri by the Montana gold boom and the Indian campaigns that followed the Civil War.

La Barge began his career in 1832 when few but keelboatmen had ever ascended the river and when the steamboat itself was in its infancy. Marsh, on the other hand, did not feel his way upstream to Fort Benton until 1866—when railheads had been established on the lower river and dozens of steamers were taking part in the summer race to the mountains. But the two men were alike in many aspects of character and attitude;

For the Indians, an invisible cargo of death

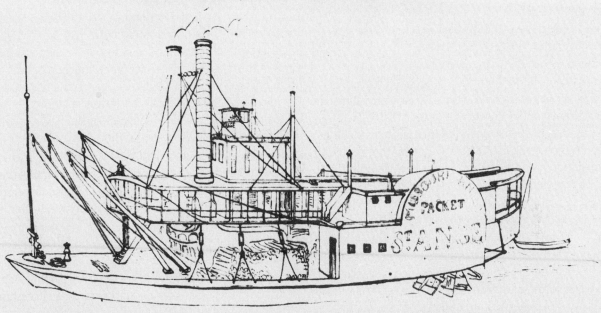

St. Ange was both blessed and cursed: in 1850 she set a speed record on the Yellowstone, but in 1851 the vessel was swept by a cholera epidemic.

In the history of the West, there was no more dangerous carrier of disease than the early steamboat with its confined spaces and fetid atmosphere. The specter of a ship-wide epidemic haunted every captain. The redoubtable Joseph La Barge underwent just such an ordeal in 1851 when his steamer, *St. Ange,* was swept by an outbreak of cholera that infected 100 passengers and crew, killing 11 before it was checked.

Nor were the dangers confined to the people on the boat. Upriver Indians had little or no resistance to many of the white man's illnesses, and contact with steamboats often had devastating results. The 1837 trip of *St. Peters* from St. Louis to Fort Union earned it an especially infamous niche in the annals of Western medicine by touching off an epidemic of smallpox that afflicted nearly every tribe from the Platte to the Rockies.

The outbreak began among the Mandans at Fort Clark when a chief stole the blanket of an infected roustabout. *St. Peters'* officers tried to retrieve it by offering a new one, and to warn the Indians away from the boat. But the Mandans, convinced that the whites were denying them the right to trade, refused to leave.

Three days after the boat's arrival the Mandans began falling sick. Hundreds died each day, their bodies swelling and turning black. Since burial of so many was impossible, the living disposed of the corpses by throwing them over cliffs — then committed suicide by the scores, preferring a quick, clean death to the grim fate unfolding before their eyes. After a few weeks, only 30 survived of a tribe that had numbered 1,700. By that time the plague was wreaking its horrors on the nearby Arikaras, Pawnees and Minnatarees.

St. Peters, meanwhile, callously pressed on upriver — there were, after all, profits to be made — and at Fort Union delivered the virus along with the cargo. The first of the Indian victims were 30 Assiniboin women who were fatally injected by a well-meaning but medically ignorant post employee with a vaccine made of the live virus. More Assiniboins came to the post to trade, and naturally caught the disease. As the stricken staggered home to die and *St. Peters* steamed home to St. Louis, smallpox spread to the Crows and Blackfeet.

By the time the smallpox plague had run its course the next year, at least 15,000 Northern Plains Indians had died of it — more than would fall in combat with the Army in the remaining 62 years of the century.

and both, above all, were helmsmen of consummate coolness, judgment and skill. La Barge never lost or even badly damaged a boat—an almost impossible record in the first years of steam—although few men made as many voyages into dangerous water as did he. Both he and Marsh were at their best in taking a steamer up unfamiliar channels, and both were admired by fellow rivermen as well as by passengers. Horace Bixby, a grand old man of the New Orleans packet trade, was in no way disturbed by a Montanan who called him "the Grant Marsh of the lower Mississippi." "By the Lord, sir," he said later, "it was a high compliment, for any man who can run a boat for 20 years on that rainwater creek above Bismarck is surely the king of pilots."

Both captains were entrepreneurs and businessmen and often had a financial interest in vessels they commanded; each was capable of handling every aspect of a boat's employment—from assessing freight rates and booking passengers to finding channels in time of low water. Neither, however, was a man who would have looked at home amid the dust of the countinghouse; upper-river captains not only had to run the gauntlet of the Missouri tribes but to preside (there being no other law for a thousand miles) over wild and undisciplined men among the passengers and crews of their steamboats. This inevitably involved a certain acceptance of violence. La Barge gave the most obstreperous of his roustabouts every chance to fight one another after his boat left St. Louis, thus easing disciplinary problems by establishing a kind of pecking order that lasted until a voyage was done. Both he and Marsh were hard men—though each met the world with a quiet and courteous air—and neither stood for any nonsense from the roughnecks who rode their steamers.

A self-proclaimed "bad man" named Gilmore did a good deal, though this was not his intention, toward instilling caution in those who dealt with Marsh after he became a captain on the upper river. Gilmore came aboard the steamer *Luella* at Fort Benton, attracted a following of noisy louts, and made life miserable for other passengers Marsh carried downstream on his first mountain voyage. He ceased his bullying after Marsh threatened to throw him off and leave him for the Indians, but publicly swore revenge. On a day when winds forced *Luella* to tie up at the bank, he announced that he was about to do so. He took his entourage

ashore, waited until Marsh followed with a woodcutting party, and cried: "Watch me make this low down dog of a captain jump the mark!" The captain went red with rage, yanked out a pistol, walked up to the bully and his grinning cronies and said, "Gilmore, the time has come. You've been looking for trouble and you're going to get it." He nodded at his would-be tormentor's revolver, waved to a space near the bank, and said, "Come over here and fight. I'll give you a fair chance."

Gilmore turned pale and began shaking his head. Marsh stepped closer, hit him across the face and yelled, "Now will you fight?" and, as the trembling man backed off, said, "I'll kill you right here if you don't!" Startled passengers moved between the pair. Marsh allowed himself to be led away and, once he had recovered his composure, began regretting the violence of his reaction. He decided, in the end, that he owed all concerned some gesture of conciliation. When the boat reached Sioux City, he followed some of his passengers, Gilmore among them, to a waterfront saloon and invited all present to advance to the bar and allow him to buy them a drink. This effort at making amends collapsed almost instantly: Gilmore sullenly refused his hospitality. The Marsh legend, however, attained new dimensions in the same moment. The exasperated host seized a heavy beer mug, and yelled, "Come up here and drink, Gilmore, or by the Eternal I'll break this glass over your skull!" He kept the impromptu weapon firmly in hand until his unwilling guest advanced amid catcalls and choked down a glass of whiskey.

News of such confrontations traveled fast along the Missouri, and so did word of unusual navigational episodes that proved a pilot's skill. Marsh became as acclaimed, in time, as La Barge himself. And La Barge was a celebrity indeed in the early West: bankers, traders, scientists and the odd Indian chief were flattered to be invited to his wheelhouse; dignitaries went out of their way to meet him on trips to St. Louis; and many of the Union generals of the Civil War became his admirers during tours of duty in Indian country. So did Mormon leader Brigham Young, Senator Thomas Hart Benton, and—on one pre-presidential trip to Council Bluffs—Honest Abe himself.

Joseph La Barge was not only a pioneer among pilots and one who made himself a model for those who followed, but was also a man whose family background and early experiences as a fur trader and Indian fighter made him a link between the French-Canadian wanderers who first explored the Missouri wilderness and the Yankee captains, miners and settlers who took it from the Indians in the end. He never lost a cold realist's eye for the wilderness through which the river led him, and never abandoned a hot, Gallic insistence on personal independence — a quality he inherited from his father, a notable riverman on his own.

The father sprang from a family of Norman peasant blood that had lived in Quebec since 1633, but he celebrated his 21st birthday, in 1808, by setting forth in a birch bark canoe to seek his fortune on the Missouri. He settled in St. Louis, served in upriver trapping expeditions, and took no back talk from any man. When a St. Louis judge fined him four dollars for caning a trapper, the old man handed over double the amount, since he proposed — as he politely informed the magistrate — to whip the fellow all over again for taking him to court, and saw no point in sitting through a second trial.

All three of his sons became steamboat pilots. All three seem to have possessed his extrasensory feel for moving water as well as his sense of command, but Joseph, the oldest, was shaped by an apprenticeship unusual even in that rough day and, having lived through it, seemed to carry some unique and permanent gift of survival with him through the rest of life.

Young Joseph began his career on the Missouri at the age of 16 as a fur trader for Pierre Chouteau Jr.'s American Fur Company, which exerted something close to dictatorship in the upper valley, and he quickly achieved a reputation for hardihood and wit. Stragglers from a Sioux war party spotted him on an open plain as he headed for a trading compound with a companion and five mules loaded with buffalo meat. He leveled his rifle and faced the Indians down while his partner whipped the loaded beasts to safety, sounded the alarm and finally returned with help. The redoubtable Etienne Provost happened to be present at the trading compound. He seized La Barge's hands and cried — as the wilderness grapevine was not slow in reporting — "I am glad you did not show the white feather to those rascals. You are a man for this country!"

La Barge won the admiration of his superiors in the company during these adventurous early years ashore and he served the firm well as a pilot and charter cap-

CHANGES OF THE CHANNEL
OF THE
MISSOURI RIVER
THROUGH MONONA COUNTY, IOWA.
Present Channel Distance, 44 Miles.
(COMPILED BY MITCHELL VINCENT, ONAWA, IOWA.)

	1804	LEWIS AND CLARK
	1852	U. S. LAND SURVEY.
	1879	MO. RIV. COM. SURVEY.
	1894	COUNTY SURVEY

tain later on. But he was audacious enough to compete with it, too. In 1840, when he was 25 years old, he quarreled with an American Fur Company official, turned down a berth in its steamboat *Trapper,* and went ashore to trade with Indians on his own. This was risky, for the company stopped at almost nothing to maintain its ascendancy and ensure its profits.

He went broke, as things turned out, and the company invited him — through the offices of an Indian runner — to a conciliatory meeting at Fort Pierre. La Barge was surprised to note that the Indian had come to his wilderness post unarmed and at once assumed that the man had been instructed to murder him after they set off together for the fort. He slipped away alone, backtracked the runner, found a rifle the fellow had hidden under some foliage, and hid it all over again. He betrayed not the slightest indignation at this duplicity,

127

A desolate depot, 60 miles from the Missouri River's last landing at Fort Benton, is heaped with supplies that will be carried by wagon train to inland trading posts. The groceries, furniture, medicine and whiskey stacked on the riverbank were brought upriver from Bismarck, North Dakota.

though he took a certain poker-faced satisfaction — after rejoining the guide — at watching the man's equally poker-faced efforts to spot the missing weapon.

La Barge regarded the company's monolithic unscrupulousness almost as philosophically as he regarded the excesses of the Sioux — or of the weather — and made a point of anticipating its dirty tricks rather than losing sleep over them. The company's men were equally realistic: they betrayed neither surprise nor disappointment at his arrival, treated him with punctilio, and bought out his trade goods at 10 cents on the dollar. But the incident did not quite end there: a band of Yanktonais Sioux — who went wild at learning he had sold out and had put them again at the mercy of the company's exorbitant prices — tried to waylay and kill him on his way home. La Barge ran 40 miles across the plains, guiding himself by the light of the aurora borealis as the temperature dropped to 30° below, before losing his pursuers near the mouth of the Cheyenne River.

La Barge had begun learning rivermanship while still engaged in the fur trade, and on one upriver trip aboard the American Fur Company's *Yellowstone,* he received a grim foretaste of the role that would make him famous. Cholera swept the boat and killed half her crew — including her pilot, her engineer and all her firemen. The captain tied up opposite Kansas' Kaw River, turned the boat over to young La Barge, climbed into the yawl with the other survivors and headed back to St. Louis to find a new crew. After the captain left, local Missouri settlers — in mortal fear of the plague — threatened to march on the vessel and set her ablaze. But La Barge fired the boilers, engaged the engine, steered her across the river and managed to tie her up in safety against the Kansas shore.

La Barge became a steamboat clerk after his youthful years as a fur trader and soon moved up to the wheelhouse as an apprentice steersman and then a pilot on the lower river. He bought the steamer *General Brooks* for $12,000 in 1846 when he was 31 years old, and built up a fortune over the years by buying, selling, building, chartering and operating other vessels. His capacity for pragmatism — and for the sardonic view — played no small part in his career as a steamboatman in the wilds. He had no quarrel at all, for example, with so elemental an aspect of the fur trade as the sale of whiskey to Indians; he was delighted, in fact — when

chartered by the American Fur Company — to outwit inspectors whom the government stationed at lower-river checkpoints to halt the liquor traffic into the Rockies. He put his whiskey barrels ashore with other freight after stopping at Bellevue, Iowa, on one upstream trip, invited the clergyman in charge of inspection to search the boat — and ordered the booze back on board after that gentleman had congratulated him on his sympathetic attitude and had retired to quarters ashore.

The famed naturalist John James Audubon helped La Barge play an even more ludicrous trick on an inspecting Army officer when they traveled upstream together on the steamer *Omega* in the spring of 1843. Steamboatmen — La Barge included — considered Audubon a pompous and overbearing ass; and Audubon, in his turn, regarded rivermen as a trying lot of simpletons and dolts. Audubon liked to drink, however, and was horrified when a young Army man put a rifle shot across *Omega*'s bows at Bellevue and waved her in to the bank to be searched. The naturalist introduced himself to the young officer, asked for the "privilege" of inspecting the post at which the man was stationed and was led, instantly, ashore and treated as a guest of honor by the camp's dazzled commandant. La Barge, who was the boat's pilot, and Joseph Sire, its captain, used the time to get their whiskey barrels below decks and loaded on a narrow-gauge tramway that ran in a circle around the shallow hold. The inspector was not only lighted down into this black tunnel by candles on his return, but was urged to crawl, at times bumping his head, around the whole circuit while roustabouts pushed the whiskey-laden cars ahead of him in the gloom.

La Barge had a much better understanding of Indians than the Army officers and Indian agents who were given the task of dealing with them; he was known and trusted, indeed, by many chiefs along the river. Yet the Sioux, who boarded and stormed his *Martha* in 1847, remained a continual source of danger. No Missouri steamer was ever subject to such persistent attack as was his chartered vessel, *Robert Campbell,* in the summer of 1863. This was a year of low water and intense tribal hostility. La Barge took the heavy-laden *Campbell* upstream with a smaller steamer, *Shreveport* — planning to cope with the first problem by transferring part of his cargo from *Campbell* to *Shreveport* when they reached the shallow upper river. He presumed, that the second problem would solve itself; he had shipments of annuity goods for the Mandans, Sioux, Crows and Blackfeet, and Indians usually swallowed their anger, at least temporarily, when it was time to line up for their peace bribes from the government.

He reckoned, however, without passenger Samuel M. Latta, an Indian agent in charge of disbursing goods for all tribes but the Blackfeet. Angry spokesmen from the Two Kettles band of Sioux came to see La Barge after he tied up at Fort Pierre, pointed out that they had received only two thirds of their goods, and—for all their friendship with the captain—demanded the rest on pain of armed retaliation. He told them the truth: that his cargo belonged to the government and that he had no control over its division among people on shore.

Peace reigned as the steamer lay at the bank, but La Barge—and everybody else aboard her—soon discovered that the Sioux meant business. When *Robert Campbell* headed upstream, the Two Kettles band mounted their horses and set out in dogged pursuit. The steamer seldom stopped for wood without enduring scattered fusillades from the angry Indians. La Barge piled cargo around the pilothouse and engine spaces and kept his attackers at a distance by arming his roustabouts and returning the fire. But the Sioux refused to give up. They chased the boat upriver for 600 miles, got ahead of her, and finally found a perfect place to wait in ambush for her arrival. The channel curved in against the bank at this spot, and no boat could pass —thanks to a long sand bar out in the stream—without moving within 30 yards of the shore.

But the fates—and a hunter named Louis Dauphin —sided this time with La Barge. Dauphin was almost as well known for his daring and woodsmanship in the golden era of the steamboats as Etienne Provost had been in the day of the mountain men. He had signed on to provide meat for *Shreveport* and *Campbell* and had been ranging the country between the big bends of the Missouri even as the Sioux had been scouring the shore. He had managed to deliver game to both boats by emerging from cover as one or the other of them caught up with him on their circuitous progress upstream. Now he moved even more surreptitiously in warning *Campbell* of the trap ahead. La Barge, still miles below the ambush, saw a hat floating oddly on the river upstream. He put his glasses on it, and presently saw it lift, slight-

ly, to reveal the hunter's head. La Barge rang his engine-room bell for stop and Dauphin pulled himself, dripping, onto the deck: "I had to take to the water. There were too many for me. You're going to have trouble. . . . There are 1,500 of them waiting."

Shreveport lay cautiously dead in the water a hundred yards below the point of ambush as *Campbell* approached; La Barge pulled slowly around her, saw his pursuers gathered en masse on the bank and stopped, too. A parley began across 60 yards of water. The Indians spoke in conciliatory tones: they wanted nothing but their rightful goods. Indian agent Latta indignantly refused. But he then asked La Barge to send his yawl to shore "for some chiefs and head men so we can talk and give them sugar and quiet them." La Barge was dumfounded by Latta's assumption that Indians willing to ride 600 miles after his steamer were not to be considered a deadly serious and dangerous lot—and refused, as indignantly, in return. "Well," said Latta, "I'm not afraid of them," and asked for the right to seek volunteers among the crew. La Barge hesitated but, staring hard at the agent, finally agreed.

Here the tale diverges as such reminiscences often do. Passenger Henry A. Boller *(page 74)* insisted afterward that members of *Campbell*'s crew ran to the opposite side of the boat as Latta turned toward them, lowered themselves over the side and hung there, refusing to go near the yawl. They acquiesced, said Boller, when the mate got an ax and "threatened to cut their fingers off."

La Barge (who denied Boller's story until his dying day) did not let the seven men aboard the yawl set off for shore until he had ordered both steamboats' cannons (two on *Campbell,* one on *Shreveport*) loaded and aimed, and had armed the crews of both vessels with rifles. Latta, watching, decided to stay behind after all—a wise, if unpraiseworthy, decision.

Several warriors waited at the water's edge as the yawl approached. When the boat ran up on the shore, they leaped in and killed three roustabouts with lances and rifles; an Indian archer, back on the shore, wounded another. The two remaining oarsmen threw themselves to the bottom of the yawl, but the steersman—a quick-witted fellow named Andy Stinger—jumped overboard, crouched behind the gunwales and tried to haul the boat away from the bank. At that point, the men back

Men who mastered the mighty Missouri

"In order to be a pilot a man had to learn more than any man ought to be allowed to know," wrote Mark Twain about the virtuoso performances demanded of riverboat pilots and captains, adding: "He must learn it all over again in a different way every 24 hours."

The captains learned the fundamentals of their craft as lowly deck hands or cabin boys. All earned renown for their ability to cope with Indians, unreliable machinery and roisterous crews as they guided their boats, according to an entry in the log of one ship, "just a little beyond no place."

Joseph LaBarge, as a youth, disqualified himself for the priesthood, confessing a great fondness for the ladies. As Captain La Barge, he was asked how he was affected by the Missouri's constant hazards. His reply: "I am actively engaged and forget the river's dangers."

Grant Marsh, a cabin boy at 12, spent a total of 32 years on the Missouri defying the river's reputation as a graveyard for steamboats. Only one vessel under his command — *Little Eagle No. 2* — was ever lost: it flipped over during a twister and sank into the Big Muddy in 1894.

Daniel Maratta, whose flamboyance and "petroleum tongue" made him a pet of the press, began as cabin boy in the 1850s and capped his career in command of *Fontanelle,* one of the fastest boats on the river, before leaving its wheel to oversee a company fleet from a desk.

Charles Blunt Sr. rose from deck hand to captain in just three years. But his fortunes turned sour as an owner. Transporting Civil War troops, he lost one boat to a boiler explosion and another in an ambush by Rebels. Congress turned a deaf ear to his loss claims.

Charles Blunt Jr., unlike most rivermen, stayed with the same company for 45 years. Imperturbable, he once rode out a tornado during which, wrote the *Bismarck Tribune*, "he stood in the pilot house as the boat's superstructure was cleaned off right behind his head."

Carrol J. Atkins, who left Vermont for the Missouri, suffered an epic humiliation in command of *Live Oak* in 1865. Seeing an alluring lady on a bluff waving her hat, he gallantly put in to shore — whereupon her hidden confederates robbed passengers and crew.

John M. Belk boarded his first steamboat when he was 13, as owner-operator of a refreshment stand. He got his first experience at the wheel five years later when he signed on *Evening Star* as errand boy and a kindly pilot allowed him to use his spare time steering the boat.

William ("Captain Billy") Sims was 27 when this photo was taken in 1869 and just establishing himself as one of the steadiest and most respected masters of the river. He began his career at the age of 15 as a cub pilot under his uncle, Captain Charles Blunt Sr.

on the steamboats, thinking that Stinger and his crew had been killed, opened up with their three cannons and small arms. The storm of shot swept the attackers away from the yawl, felling nearly 40 Sioux and 20 horses in all.

Steersman Stinger managed to get the yawl into open water by paddling furiously with one hand, climbed back into it, and directed its two unwounded oarsmen toward the sand bar. Both leaped out on arrival there, and Stinger was left—cursing brilliantly—to bring the boat, its dead men and wounded survivor, back to the steamer by himself. But that was the end of the Indians' long chase. The runaway crewmen were retrieved, the Sioux further discouraged with cannon fire, and *Campbell* churned on to the mouth of the Yellowstone with passengers, crew, corpses and freight.

This battle reflected a new belligerency on the part of Indians. Missouri tribes had not regarded white men as real threats to their hunting grounds during the years of the fur trade, and Indians who fired at passing vessels had usually done so out of individual pique, or as a matter of casual sport. But Montana gold—which prospectors began discovering at Gold Creek and Bannack in 1862—was already altering these attitudes and this state of affairs when the Two Kettles band was moved to its anguished if angry feud with *Campbell*.

Gold drew hundreds and then thousands of miners to camps like Virginia City and Last Chance Gulch and threatened the last, vast Indian domains as a few scattered trappers had never done. It turned bands of Sioux and Northern Cheyennes into impassioned enemies who harassed steamers and Army posts alike, and did so as a matter of principle and on every possible occasion. Gold, too, finished the era of lonely mountain voyages that Joseph La Barge so typified, and launched a new era of massive upper-river traffic and of steamer-assisted military campaigns.

This is not to say that La Barge failed to respond with ardor and alacrity to the new chances for wealth that gold so suddenly provided shippers and traders. His organization of La Barge, Harkness & Company —to which he and his brother John and three St. Louis investors each contributed $10,000 in 1862—was an ambitious but perfectly logical reaction to new times in Montana. The firm proposed to deal in annuities and take goods of its own upstream—as well as cargo for

customers—and to sell them at big profits in mining camps. But La Barge and his associates soon became mired in financial disasters. La Barge's partner, James Harkness, took a wagon-train load of the firm's goods to the Deer Lodge Valley in one instance, and then —startled by life among whiskery miners—turned it over to a sharp trader named Nick Wall and hurried back to his fireside in St. Louis. Wall—a Confederate sympathizer whom La Barge had extricated from federal authorities in Missouri, and whom he had grubstaked and given free passage upriver—then sold the consignment, kept the money and embroiled his benefactor in a long, costly and losing damage suit in the Montana courts. The company ultimately collapsed—having cost La Barge $100,000.

He set forth alone to retrieve his fortunes and made a gallant fight of it. He scraped up $40,000 to buy a three-quarters interest in the steamboat *Effie Deans* in 1864, took a cargo of mining supplies upstream, turned the boat over to his brother John when it was stalled by low water, rounded up wagons, drivers and oxen and took his goods on to Fort Benton and Virginia City by land. This venture in trading left him the possessor of $100,000 in gold dust—and made him a target of opportunity for the gangs of road agents that spied on well-heeled men in the gold fields and robbed them if they attempted to travel beyond. La Barge reserved a seat on an eastbound stagecoach (which highwaymen duly stopped and searched), but sneaked safely out of town a day early on another stage bound for Salt Lake City. He dropped in on his old friend, Brigham Young, bought a team and wagon, drove it into the valley of the Platte, hid for days on a river island to avoid an Indian war party, got back to the Missouri with his treasure—having traveled 8,400 miles since spring—and boarded the season's last downstream vessel for home.

La Barge brought back $50,000 in gold dust from another personal trading venture the following year. But *Effie Deans* then burned to the water line at the levee in St. Louis, and La Barge, whose stubborn sense of honor precluded his taking any other course, used much of his newly gained profit and his remaining energies in settling debts that haunted him in his declining years. He remained a figure of patriarchal authority on the river until he was 70, and a celebrity on the streets of St. Louis until he died in 1899 at the age of 84.

Grant Marsh would prove a worthy heir to La Barge's mantle as the Missouri's premier pilot and captain; but the motley citizenry of Fort Benton was hardly aware of him or his steamboat *Luella* when he tied up there on June 17, 1866, to discharge a cargo of groceries and mining machinery and to loose a cabinful of argonauts upon the wilderness. Rich gold strikes, coinciding with Lee's distant surrender at Appomattox, had triggered such waves of invasion and exploitation as the northern Rockies had never known, and the Montana gold boom was roaring in earnest at last. Thirty-one steamers had reached, or were approaching, the head of navigation—though not more than a half dozen had done so in any previous year—and they now lay bow to stern along a half mile of riverfront. Huge freight wagons stood in Fort Benton's rutted lanes; and its shabby bars and dance halls were jammed with plainsmen, unfrocked Confederate soldiers, Mexicans, Missouri, plowboys and miners.

But Marsh, though only 34 years old and making his first voyage as a captain, was not a man who went unheeded in any company. He was a clear-eyed and open young man with an easy manner and a deceptively soft voice; but he was, as well, a big, lean, hard-muscled fellow who wore an unmistakable air of decision and command. His *Luella* made history before the summer was over.

Marsh had never laid eyes on the upper reaches of the river before feeling his way to Fort Benton in *Luella*. But that was lesson enough. In the same season, he took his steamer back through its shoals and rapids twice again after discharging his original cargo—once to rescue the passengers and machinery of a steamer wrecked in white water 70 miles downstream, and once to aid in closing up the old fur-trading post of Fort Union at the mouth of the Yellowstone. And, having done so, he made a decision that reflected that ultimate quality of great pilots: an intuitive ability to see some constricted but logical route through water others considered wholly dangerous; and beyond that, the confidence to assume that, in the end, almost any stretch of river would be negotiable, given time and resolution.

Captains made a practice of turning their boats around after unloading at Fort Benton and of heading downstream in a hurry to avoid entrapment by the shallowing water of midsummer. But Marsh, having kept *Luella* at work on the upper river into August, decided to delay until September—although she was the last vessel at the riverbank—and thus to accommodate crowds of miners who wished to stay at the diggings as long as possible before taking their earnings home. His mind made up, he headed into the Highwood Mountains and hunted deer for a week with a party of his officers and passengers-to-be. *Luella* headed for home, as a result of her late departure, with the most valuable cargo ever borne downstream: $1,250,000 in gold dust. And she collected an impressive weight of the precious metal for herself in the process.

Miners paying for tickets in dust made a practice of debasing it with sand, but Marsh had heard of this ruse during the summer; he countered it by making every passenger pan his offering clean before weighing out the price of a voyage to St. Louis. *Luella* delivered them there with remarkable ease and dispatch, though she was bushwhacked near the mouth of the Milk River by Indians, who found her stuck on a sand bar and began firing down at her from the summit of a high bluff. Marsh simply called his 230 passengers to the deck with their shooting irons and drove the tribesmen off the skyline with the first, noisy fusillade. He got boat, passengers, gold and crew to St. Louis without further incident. He had worked *Luella* as few boats had ever been worked on the upper river, had handily disposed of an Indian war party, and made a profit of $24,000 in the bargain—all of which earned him a respect rarely accorded new captains on the Missouri.

Marsh was more firmly grounded in the fundamentals of paddle navigation than a good many of his new admirers realized. He had been working on the Western rivers for 22 years, having run away from his parents' home near Pittsburgh to become a cabin boy on the Allegheny River steamer, *Dover*. He had served as a stripling roustabout and as a husky young mate on the Ohio, the Mississippi, the Tennessee and the lower Missouri; and had lived through the great St. Louis "ice gorge" of 1856. There were few "trades"—commercial runs—on any of the Western waters in which he had not handled cargo or commanded deck crews.

Marsh served as mate of the New Orleans packet *John J. Roe* that supported General Ulysses S. Grant's forces at the Battle of Shiloh on the Tennessee River in 1862. *John J. Roe* was celebrated for lack of speed

The accidental conquest of the Cascades

By every yardstick of size or traffic, the Missouri was the greatest of Western waterways, but the Columbia—churning 1,210 miles through the Pacific Northwest—ran a strong second with its burden of fur trappers, prospectors, settlers and freight. Unfortunately, traffic on it was blocked at several points by stretches of white water that confined a steamboat to the section of river on which it was built. Passengers and cargo had to be unloaded to bypass these rapids via portage railway and then resume the journey on relay boats.

One of the deadliest of the foaming obstructions was the Cascades, a six-mile gauntlet of rocks midway between a town called The Dalles and Portland, Oregon. From the first appearance of steamers on the Columbia River in 1836, pilots regarded the Cascades as a sure deathtrap; but in 1858 the stern-wheeler *Venture* proved them wrong. Her pilot, setting off upstream from above the rapids, failed to call for enough steam and the boat was swept back over the rapids stern first. Incredibly, *Venture* fetched up in calm water with all hands safe—but for one hapless soul who had panicked, leaped overboard and drowned.

This lucky accident coincided with the growth of Portland as a major shipping center. Emboldened by the news that the Cascades could be crossed, shipowners operating above it encouraged their captains to shoot the rapids —bow first—and join the Portland-to-Pacific trade.

Prudent pilots tackled the Cascades when the water was high; but in 1888 one of the most renowned captains on

White-water champion James Troup

the river, James W. Troup, dared to make the run at low water in the 462-ton *Hassalo*. On the great day—May 26—thousands of thrill seekers gathered to watch the bold Troup do or die. Photographers snapped and supporters cheered lustily as *Hassalo (left)* barreled through the obstacle course in a breathtaking seven minutes and wound up with only minor scrapes. Troup moved on to seek new challenges in British Columbia, and eight years later a canal-and-lock system was built to end forever the hazard of the Cascades.

An act of Congress in 1852 made pilots' licenses mandatory. Its aim, stated in small print, was to "provide for the better security of the lives of passengers on board vessels propelled in whole or in part by steam."

("so slow," wrote Mark Twain in *Life on the Mississippi,* "that when she finally sank in Madrid Bend it was five years before the owners heard of it."). She was, however, one of the largest boats on the river and was used to move two complete regiments of Union infantry from the captured bastion of Fort Donelson to Pittsburgh Landing, 300 miles upstream. The armies fought close to the river there — 55,000 Union soldiers trying to dislodge 42,000 Confederates from the key position at Shiloh Church. Marsh watched in admiration as a furious officer of General Grant's staff stopped an incipient retreat at pistol point — and he saw a man standing within a few feet of him on deck decapitated by a Confederate cannon ball. Every man aboard *John J. Roe* knew the price paid for Shiloh Church; she took 600 wounded soldiers with her when she headed back to St. Louis. The Union forces had suffered 13,000 casualties overall, and the Confederacy nearly as many.

Marsh was guided in later life by impressions formed during these thunderous and bloody days: by an admiration for good soldiers and a sense of duty to them, and by a personal belief in the efficacy of daring and resolution during moments of stress or danger. These traits were mandatory on the Missouri during the years of gold boom in Montana and Idaho, for the Sioux reacted with savage bitterness to the encroachment of white travelers and soldiers. Red Cloud, the great Oglala Sioux war chief, besieged Forts Kearny, Reno and C. F. Smith so successfully in 1866 and 1867 that the government was forced to close the Bozeman Road — the overland emigrant route from the North Platte River to Virginia City, Montana.

With east-west travel thus confined to the Missouri, other warriors harassed the miserable little log-built posts the Army established on the upper river. Sitting Bull of the Hunkpapa band waged a kind of psychological warfare on the garrison at Fort Buford in the winter of 1867; he not only bottled its shivering soldiers inside its walls for months, but kept his warriors banging continuously on a circular saw, captured from the post's sawmill, to dramatize his presence outside the fort's log stockade.

This hostility was extended to steamers when and if they could be attacked from the shore. Marsh, having weathered one ambush in *Luella,* was compelled to cope with another and more serious attack when he took the steamboat *Ida Stockdale* to Fort Benton the following year.

The Sioux liked heights, since the vulnerable wooden roofs of armored wheelhouses were exposed to snipers firing from above. *Ida Stockdale* ran into trouble at a point where an island divided the river and pushed the steamer channel close to the north bank under a precipice known as Plenty Coal Bluff. A big war party — which had been riding along the south shore when they saw the vessel's smoke — divided to waylay her. Dozens of horsemen swam their mounts across the river and scrambled up the bluff; others crossed to the island; and the rest — just in case — stayed where they were. No steamer had ever chanced the fast, narrow chute between the island and the southern bank; but Marsh, watching the hurried deployment of the Indians, decided to risk it — and accept gunfire aimed at river level rather than expose the boat to fusillades from on high. He headed into the quickening water of the chute, scraped across a sand bar with bullets clanging on his boiler plate, put his wheel hard down to avoid a jutting snag, ground along the bottom for awful seconds — and glided into open water beyond the island with the sound of Indian musketry dying into frustrated silence astern.

There was a curious inconsistency about these brushes with Indians and, indeed, about the whole pattern of their reaction to whites. Almost all bands took recesses in enmity at times, and the captain who came downstream with bullet holes in his upper works might find himself starting back with cargo for the very warriors who had put them there. Marsh attached less importance to his adventure at Plenty Coal Bluff than to the fact that he had made a profit of $24,000 during the voyage on which it occurred. And he agreed, the following year — when the government asked him to deliver annuities it had pledged in making peace with Red Cloud — to one of the most outlandish proposals ever put to a riverman: to risk almost certain freeze-up by taking the steamer *Nile* upstream in October with cargo for an Indian agency at the mouth of the Grand River in Dakota Territory.

One can only speculate about those aspects of character that prompted Marsh to attempt this difficult project. He was intensely proud of his skill at the wheel. He also had reason to expect that his attempt to get up-

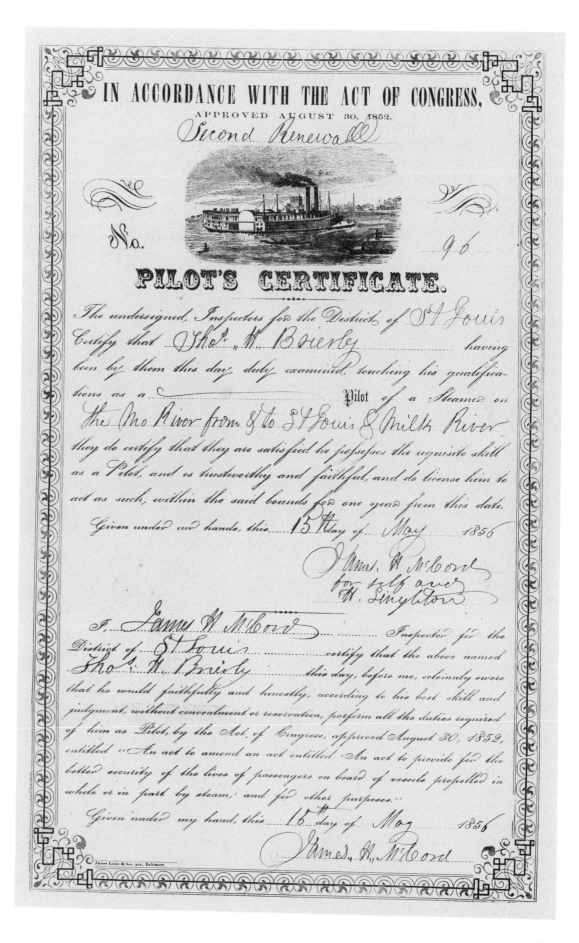

IN ACCORDANCE WITH THE ACT OF CONGRESS,

APPROVED AUGUST 30, 1852.

Second Renewal

No.

96

PILOT'S CERTIFICATE.

The undersigned, Inspectors for the District of *St Louis*
Certify that *Thos. W. Boierly* having
been by them this day, duly examined, touching his qualifica-
tions as a _____ Pilot of a Steamer on
the Mo River from & to St Louis & Milk River
they do certify that they are satisfied he possesses the requisite skill
as a Pilot, and is trustworthy and faithful, and do license him to
act as such, within the said bounds for one year from this date.

Given under our hands, this *15* day of *May* 1856

James H McCord
for self and
H Singleton

I, *James H McCord* _____ Inspector for the
District of *St Louis* _____ certify that the above named
Thos. W. Briely _____ this day, before me, solemnly swore
that he would faithfully and honestly, according to his best skill and
judgment, without concealment or reservation, perform all the duties required
of him as Pilot, by the Act of Congress, approved August 30, 1852,
entitled "An act to amend an act entitled 'An act to provide for the
better security of the lives of passengers on board of vessels propelled in
whole or in part by steam,' and for other purposes."

Given under my hand, this *15* day of *May* 1856

James H McCord

James Lucas & Son, prs. Baltimore.

river would be construed as an act of patriotism by the Quartermaster Department of the Army on which the burden of delivery had been placed; and he was shrewd enough to realize that there was profit for the steamboatman who retained the good graces of governmental agencies. But it is hard not to believe that he was attracted as well by the risky drama of the proposal. The odds against his returning before spring were astronomical and no steamer had previously weathered a winter on the upper river. Marsh seems, however, to have remembered his earlier escapes from ice; to have felt that a vessel could live if frozen into protected water; and to have looked forward, with a certain curiosity, to exile in the wilderness. *Nile,* at any rate, became the first steamer to endure freeze-up and return unscathed. Marsh fell far short of the Grand River: low water forced him to secrete part of his cargo on an island just above Yankton and to unload the rest at the mouth of the Cheyenne River. But he got less than 100 miles back downstream before closing ice forced him to choose a mooring against the east bank and there await the coming of warmer weather.

Nile came to rest near an encampment of Lower Brulé Indians, a particularly unruly lot of Sioux. This band was so intent on staying warm, however, and so dependent on supplies from the agency at Fort Thompson, that it saw no profit in wading through snow to raid a well-armed and empty steamboat. Marsh, as a result, was able to devote himself to heroic walking expeditions along the frozen river. He made frequent hikes to Fort Thompson, which lay 20 miles from the boat, and took longer excursions almost weekly: 47 miles to the island on which he had stored his cargo and 47 miles back the next day.

Men from the Indian agency were abashed, and a little nettled, to discover — on accompanying him back to the boat on one occasion — that they simply could not match strides with him. They sought to even the psychological score with frontier humor and asked him to dinner at the fort, where they slyly served him a "special dish" of stewed dog. Marsh assumed it was venison and ate with such relish — though those around him confined themselves to bacon — that his host could not bring himself to confess until 38 years later.

The captain's victims now sought a hiker who could outwalk him over the 47 miles to Cul-de-sac Island.

To relieve boredom on the Big Muddy, passengers were at times encouraged to go ashore under guard and admire the countryside. This party was led by Captain John Belk *(second from left)*, and included M. L. Marsh, the great Grant Marsh's younger brother *(center rear)*, a first-rate engineer.

Steamboat Captain Minnie Hill

First lady of the Columbia

When 20-year-old Minnie Mossman married Columbia River Captain Charles Hill in 1883 she meant to be more than a mere mate to him. Joining Charles in the pilothouse, she learned the river currents and skills of boat-handling so well that in 1886 she was able to astound two skeptical inspectors with her expertise — and become the first licensed female steamboat captain west of the Mississippi. For the next three years the Hills operated a ramshackle trader boat on the lower Columbia. Then, in 1889, they purchased the 112-foot stern-wheeler *Governor Newell* to haul freight downriver — with Captain Minnie in command and Charles in the engine room answering her bells. In time, the couple acquired four more boats and a baby son. The boy lived aboard *Newell* until 1900, when Minnie moved ashore with him so that he could go to school. But whenever a Hill boat was short a captain, the enterprising Minnie filled in — still unchallenged as the Columbia River's only woman at the wheel.

An agency Indian named Bad Moccasin was nominated for the contest but fell behind, panting, after only an hour. One Dutch Jake — a laborer at the fort — went the distance but finished two miles behind. Some Lower Brulé Indians then suggested a genuine prodigy — a skinny little Sioux called Fast Walker — and his services were duly enlisted.

Fast Walker, it developed, did not walk at all; he ran. He vanished from Marsh's sight after only a few miles, trotted blithely to the island, ran 20 miles more, rolled up in a blanket for a few hours, and then ran another 70 miles to visit some relatives who were camped farther along the river. Marsh accepted defeat with good humor and was on hand to applaud, during a layover the next summer, when Fast Walker took on a thoroughbred horse and beat it, too, while covering 24 miles between the fort and American Creek.

Marsh won the friendship and admiration of an increasing number of Army men in the West — and not only of the quartermasters who were indebted to him for this winter voyage in *Nile*. There was a certain dash about him that appealed to line officers — as did his skill, hardihood and good sense. And he had a way of associating himself with their problems that, in their minds, separated him from other civilians. Marsh ran big risks for mundane, but enormously appreciated, ends during October of 1869: he chanced another entrapment by ice with the steamboat *North Alabama* to deliver winter supplies of vegetables to all the forts along the river. This mission inspired an almost feverish gratitude in men who were prepared to face Indians without complaint but were absolutely appalled at the prospect of living until spring on a diet consisting of only hardtack and salt meat.

Marsh had been earning the princely sum of $1,200 a month as a captain and pilot, but in 1871 he became party to a steamboat combine as an investor in his own right. His contacts with the Army lent new dimensions to his career; they not only provided increasingly remunerative charters and cargo contracts for the line's fleet vessels, but made him a really fabled figure in U.S. military history.

Marsh was one of eight captains, financiers and shippers who created the Coulson Packet Line, a principal instrument by which the Army moved troops and supplies into Indian territory; and his services, in particular,

An 1872 receipt for goods freighted on *Nellie Peck,* commanded by Grant Marsh, lists furs sent from Fort Benton to Sioux City — a rare cargo for its time, since the fur trade had virtually died in the 1860s.

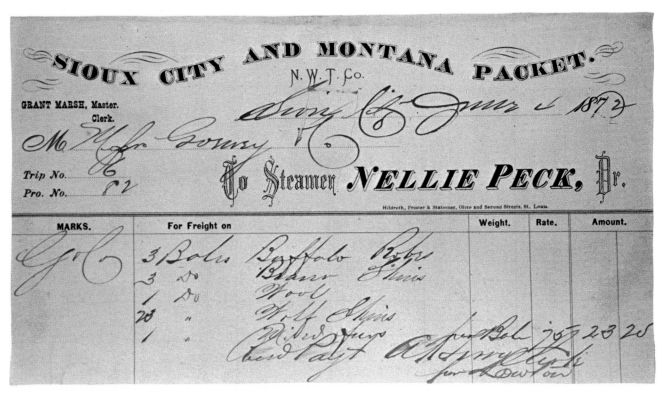

were coveted by officers charged with carrying out ticklish amphibious missions. These expeditions grew more crucial and more dangerous with the passage of time. Red Cloud and his free-roaming Sioux had been granted possession of all country "north of the North Platte River and east of the summits of the Big Horn Mountains" after their bloody closure of the Bozeman Road. But the pressure of white immigration was making this treaty agreement less tenable by the month. Chiefs Gall, Black Moon and Crazy Horse began preaching anew the gospel of the warpath, the government moved the 7th Cavalry under George Custer into Fort Abraham Lincoln as a counterthreat, and the Army began preparing itself for inevitable and final conflict in southern Montana and northern Wyoming.

It was obvious that the Yellowstone River would be a key to military operations against the Sioux. Its tributaries watered the heart of the Indians' remaining hunting grounds. But the Yellowstone presented the Army with a dilemma: generations of trappers and explorers had walked its banks, and surveyors for the Northern Pacific Railroad had penetrated its valley in plotting a route to the coast, yet no man knew whether the stream was navigable for more than a few miles above its

mouth. Lieutenant General Phillip H. (Little Phil) Sheridan, the Civil War hero who now commanded the Army's Division of the Missouri, chose Marsh to explore it by steamboat: 460 miles to the mouth of the Powder River in 1873, and up vastly greater distances of its higher reaches in 1875.

These two expeditions marked the chutes and channels through which troops were ferried and supplied before, during and after the tragic Battle of the Little Bighorn in 1876. Both of them penetrated country marked "hostile" on Army maps and did not go upstream without deckloads of escorting infantrymen. But neither voyage, for all these military trappings, heard so much as an unfriendly rifle shot. They were essentially exercises — though, indeed, ultimate exercises — in river navigation and both turned, almost completely, on the skill, judgment and experience of Grant Marsh.

Key West, the Coulson steamer assigned to the first expedition, seemed to have come to the end of her voyage almost as soon as she turned into the Yellowstone on the morning of May 6, 1873. The water was very low and Marsh found himself facing a labyrinth of shallows and sand bars that spread from shore to shore. He set forth in *Key West's* yawl to seek some semblance

145

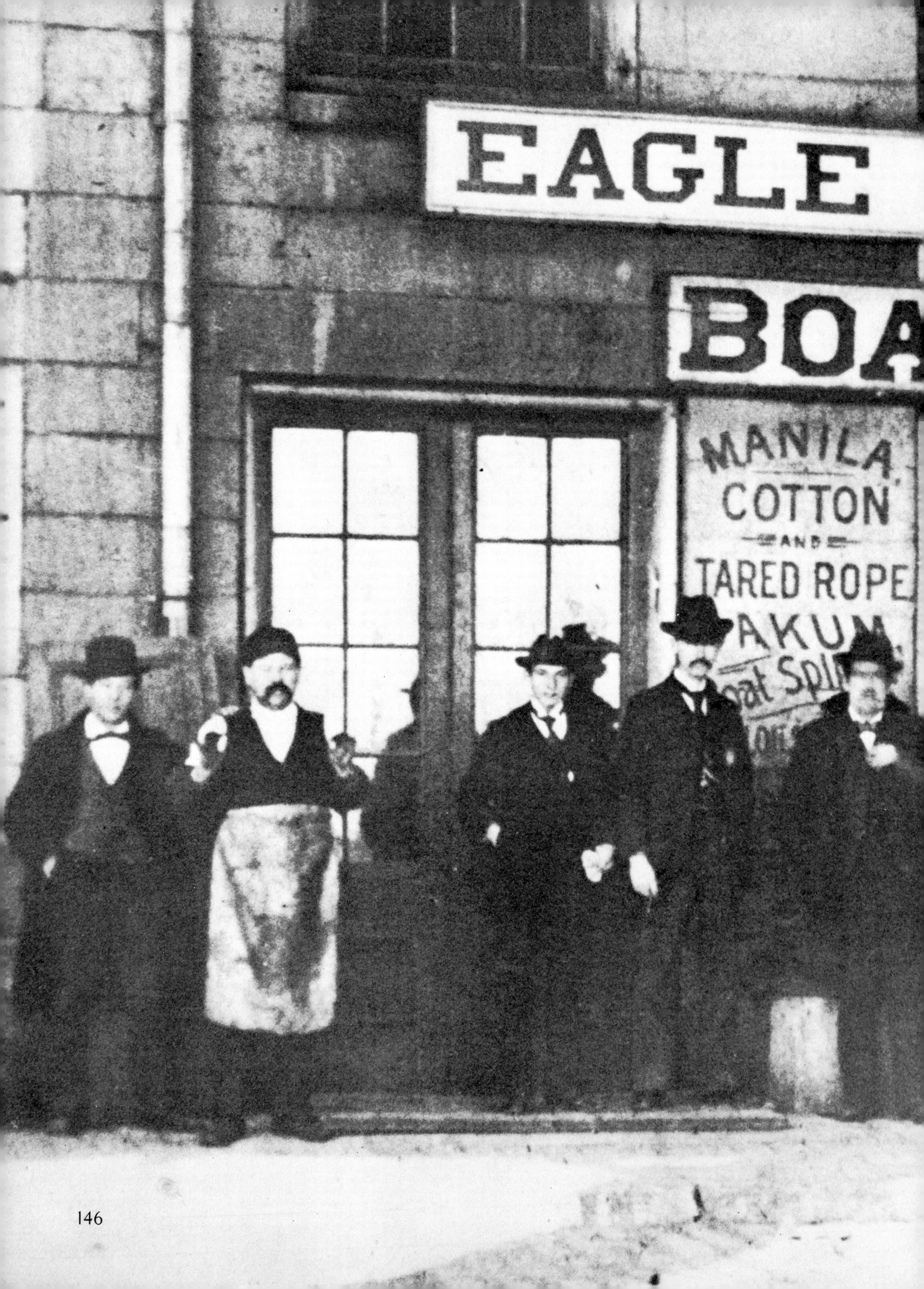
EAGLE
BOA
MANILA
COTTON
AND
TARED ROPE

On the St. Louis waterfront in the 1880s, captains and pilots meet in front of a favorite hangout between voyages. Emporiums like this were vital social centers, where boatmen traded gossip and news of available commands.

A ship company's ledger lists steamboat crews' salaries in the 1890s, by which time railroad competition had hit their wallets. Pilots were earning $125 a month, compared with $725 in the flush 1860s.

of a channel—not, in this case, water deep enough to float his vessel but simply water that would permit her some essential buoyancy as she was sparred over obstructions. He got her through, only to find similar shallows and to repeat the exasperating process a few miles farther on. These bars finally gave way not only to definite channels but to sharp rock reefs as well. And there were other hindrances to progress: generations of Indian ponies had grazed on the green bark of cottonwood trees along the stream and had so thinned, stunted and killed them that fuel was hard to find.

Marsh was soon convinced, for all this, that the Yellowstone was indeed navigable and that a good pilot could be expected to compensate for its dangers and difficulties in the future. The river's banks were stable, and the scattered pieces of driftwood that had been stranded along them at high water promised summer levels that would make its channels feasible for shallow-draft steamers. They were channels, moreover, that would not shift. The stream bed was mostly composed of gravel, and its bars—though they could tear out a vessel's bottom—were immovable obstructions that, once charted and memorized, could be avoided by a man who knew his business.

Marsh was as charmed as his crew and his two companies of soldiers at the vistas that opened before the steamer as she churned cautiously upstream. The riverside willows were turning green; vast herds of buffalo moved on the rising prairies; and elk and antelope wandered in herds, like cattle, across bottom land near the water. The boat boasted the presence of an eminent guide and hunter: Luther S. (Yellowstone) Kelly, a New Yorker who in his youth had headed to the frontier for adventure, awed the Sioux with his daring, and had coursed the West for years with "Old Sweetness," his trusty rifle. The boat's company dined on venison that Kelly shot during jaunts ashore. They named points along the stream for one another, their wives and friends: Forsyth Butte, Mary Island, De Russy Rapids. And *Key West* did her work more nimbly than anyone had believed possible: she went to the mouth of the Powder and back to the Missouri in just nine days.

This lighthearted sense of holiday was prolonged: George Custer and his 7th Cavalry were ordered into the Yellowstone valley to escort a party of railroad surveyors, and Marsh was asked to take his vessel back up-

stream as a supply boat for the horse soldiers and their flamboyant commander. Custer's support of the Northern Pacific involved sharp little clashes with Indians during the summer and was—with his subsequent reconnaissance of the Black Hills—instrumental in rousing the Sioux against the Army in 1876. The boat was not involved in these skirmishes, however, and Custer behaved, despite them, as though he were engaged in some grandiose sporting expedition. The cavalry, at one point, kept the vessel waiting in the river for two weeks; but its commander sent his regimental band ahead and the musicians, who came aboard as soon as they dismounted, played a crashing concert for captain, crew and the silent hills by the light of a summer moon. Three packs of hounds—one owned by Lord Clifford, an Englishman whom Custer brought along as a guest—came into the valley with the troops. The dogs, having been equipped with little moccasins to protect their paws from the thorns of prickly pear, were sent baying off after jack rabbits when their masters relaxed between bouts of military duty.

Two summers later, Phil Sheridan ordered Marsh into the farthest reaches of the river on another exploratory expedition. He explained in a letter: "It may be necessary, at some time in the immediate future, to occupy by a military force the country in and about the mouths of the Tongue River and the Big Horn." Since there was a possibility of trouble from the Sioux, the steamboat *Josephine* carried 100 soldiers of the 6th Infantry, four mounted scouts and a one-inch Gatling gun with 10,000 rounds of ammunition. But this voyage, too, though it penetrated hundreds of miles of unknown water and skirted hills plumed with the smoke of distant Indian signal fires, evolved into a peaceful, even dreamy summer idyl. It presented Marsh with chains of navigational problems, but it also presented him with splendid water and splendid weather as he encountered them; he thus had every possible means of dramatizing his own remarkable talent at the wheel. *Josephine* came into the Yellowstone at the peak of its spring flood and not only passed serenely over the sand bars that had delayed *Key West* in 1873, but steamed all the way to the Powder River without once having to set her spars or to warp upstream with her steam capstans.

Marsh had doubts as to what he would encounter as *Josephine* passed beyond this point and into water no

PORTAGE BOOK.

NAME.	OCCUPATION.	No. Days.	Wages per Month.	AMOUNT.		Amount Retained.	Amount Paid.
R. F. Woolfolk	Master	30	125	125			
Chas N Blunt	Clerk & Pilot	30	125	125			
Jno Bress	Pilot	30	100	100			
Ole Strom	Engineer	30	100	100			
Harry Larson	Watchman	36½	35	42	60		
Jas Thompson	Mate	30	50	50			
M. S. Moore	Carpenter	30	50	50			
Geo Fraten	Cook	5½	50	9	13		
		23½	50	38	85		
Ole Nelson	"	5	20	3	35		
Thos Moore	Cabin	33	18	19	80		
Jay Fosdick	"	36½	18	21	90		
Fannie Davis	Chambermaid	34½	18	20	70		
Dan Johns	Fireman	19½	30	19	50		
Phillip Furber	"	26	30	26			
Hugh McLaughlin	Engineer	25½	60	51			
Peter Martin	Rooster	17	30	17			
Jos Quinn	"	4½	30	4	50		
E. Lindeman	"	17	30	17			
W. E. Wilson	"	3	30	3			
H. Hendrickson	"	26½	30	26	50		
C. Mason	"	17	30	17			
Con Mahoney	"	3½	30	3	50		
L. Johnson	"	26½	30	26	50		
R. Nick	"	26½	30	26	50		
Geo Williams	"	26½	30	26	50		
Christ Putlok	"	26½	30	26	50		
Wm Glisfen	"	3	30	3			
Nick Hill	"	10½	30	10	50		
P. Schwartz	"	3½	30	3	50		
Andrew Johnson	"	26½	30	26	50		
Gilbert Gullerson	"	13½	30	13	50		
Sam Burgier	"	1½	30	1	50		
Henry Fowler	"	4	30	4			
Jno Powers	"	2½	30	2	50		
Jos Binford	"	10	30	10			
Jas Savage	"	4	30	4			
Geo Clark	"	13	30	13			
Jno Hersby	"	8½	30	8	50		
A. A. Gilett	"	1½	30	1	50		
Wm Briggs	"	1½	30	1	50		
Geo Shipley	"	9½	30	9	50		
Robt Powers	"	9	30	9			
Albert Surland	"	3½	30	3	50		
Wm Boggs	"	3½	30	3	50		
Willis Doan	"	3½	30	3	50		
R. Vassel	"	6	30	6			
Wm Pollett	"	6	30	6			
Wm Hiscock	"	6	30	6			
Wm Briggs	"	6	30	6			
C N Blunt in port.	"	5½	60	11			
				1163	33		

pilot had ever seen. But the river led on and on through
usable if reef-bordered channels, and its valley grew
more beautiful with every passing day. The steamboat
sighted one Sioux encampment on shore but had only
the briefest look at its inhabitants: they fled so pre-
cipitously that they left their tipi fires burning. The
sparse and stunted trees of the lower valley gave way to
great stands of enormous cottonwoods, some as much
as six feet through the trunk. Wooded islands appeared
in midstream. "They are so handsome," wrote General
James W. Forsyth, the Army commander on board,
"that they almost make the voyager believe he is seeing
the well kept grounds of an English country house."
Draws and bottom lands along the stream were choked
with wild plums, cherries, gooseberries, currants and
strawberries; and the prairies were alive, at times, with
herds of migrating buffalo. Soldiers and crew feasted
on wild fruit and on fresh meat from the rifle of hunter
Charley Reynolds. A sense of timelessness—of sa-
voring Eden—settled over all aboard as *Josephine*
churned, day after day, up dazzling, sunlit reaches of
water toward the retreating horizons of an untracked
and smiling world.

Marsh, for all this, kept a painstaking record of the
marks at which he aimed his steamboat and of the meth-
odology by which he moved her up the river: "Run left
hand shore up past big bluff. Plenty of dead timber at
this bend. Then cross from the deadwood to the left
hand bluff over a short, right hand bend, then circle out
between two islands (first named Crittenden Island for
General T. L. Crittenden, 17th Inf.; second named
Elk Island) and come back to a right hand prairie bend."
He did not pass the mouth of the Bighorn River without pushing up it, too, for a few miles and scribbling similar instructions to himself. Marsh kept this detailed log
for very personal reasons: to ensure his own primacy as
a pilot on the Yellowstone. He had no idea that the
Army would judge it the one most valuable by-product
of the whole expedition, would demand it from him and
would parcel out copies to the captains of other steamers it eventually chartered.

The river grew gradually faster, gradually narrower,
and finally, 27 miles above the Bighorn, squeezed its
clear, green flood into an 85-foot-wide channel between
towering and intractable cliffs. *Josephine* plunged into
this enormous millrace, slowed and hung motionless

with her paddles thrashing madly. She did not fall back,
but she could not move forward, and Marsh was forced,
while his engines labored at high pressure and his deck
hands toiled frantically with derricks and capstans, to
set spars and inch ahead, reset them and inch a little farther and to repeat the process amid the racing water for
hour after hour as rock walls sent back echoes of his vessel's banging exhaust. But *Josephine* and all aboard her
were rewarded when she emerged at last. Easier water
lay ahead, and on the horizon was a sight even Marsh
had not hoped to see: Pompey's Pillar—the lone, towering, sandstone butte that Lewis and Clark had discovered and celebrated 69 years earlier.

Marsh tied up at its base in the early afternoon, gave
soldiers and crew the rest of the day ashore, and—on
noting the legend, "Wm. Clark, July 25, 1806,"
carved on the pillar's face—climbed it himself, erected a
makeshift pole and raised one of the boat's two U.S.
flags to the gentle Montana breeze. *Josephine* labored
on for two more days and 46 more miles, sparring or
warping almost continuously through faster and faster
water. Forsyth and Marsh finally called it quits at the
head of a savage stretch of rock and foam the crew chris-
tened Hell Roaring Rapids. The pilot went ashore with
an ax and a knife, chopped a blaze on the trunk of a
huge cottonwood, and carved, "Josephine, June 7,
1875." The boat had come 483 miles upstream to a
point within 60 miles of modern Yellowstone National
Park—a feat no other steamer was ever to duplicate.

Marsh turned her around at two in the afternoon, and
—exhilarated by success, by the clear summer flood the
river still provided and, apparently, by some kind of hyp-
notic communion with his own skills—sent her swiftly
reeling back through the upper rapids, the cliff-bordered
narrows and the turbulent reaches below them at a pace
that seemed, to some of her soldiers, like flying. This
marvelous use of rudders and engines went on: *Josephine* averaged more than 100 miles between each
sunup and sundown on her downstream journey and
slid back into the Missouri River, without having so
much as touched a shoal or bar, in just four days. But
Grant Marsh had no way of knowing that he had simply conducted a rehearsal for tragedy, that time was
closing in on him—and on his friend George Custer—or
that sorrow, danger and real fame still awaited him on
the river he now knew better than any man alive.

The fateful intrusion of the "fire canoe"

To the captains who plied the upper Missouri, the Indians along the shore were a perfidious lot who might be grateful consignees one day and bloodthirsty bushwhackers the next. But to the Indians the awesome steamboats embodied all the fears and frustrations linked to the white man's presence.

The first "fire canoes" brought the Indians not only useful goods and gaudy trinkets, but also the illegal whiskey —and the deadly diseases that wreaked havoc among tribesmen, who had no natural immunity to them. Later on the vessels carried in settlers, then soldiers who crushed resistance. Finally, it was the steamboats that took the vanquished to reservations, where they were sustained by riverborne government supplies—regularly pilfered by un-scrupulous traders and corrupt agents.

Artist William Cary, who sketched these deceptively placid scenes on a trip to the upper Missouri in 1861, caught the moods of defiance, hope and resignation among the Indians, who by then had come to regard the steamboat —according to a perceptive commentator—as a symbol of "friend and foe, truth and falsehood, honor and shame."

Watched by a gesturing brave, a stern-wheeler steams through a herd of migrating buffalo that might take hours to cross the river.

153

A crowd of curious Mandans — one of a dozen tribes served by trading posts on the upper Missouri — lines the riverbank at Fort Berthold to watch a steamboat arrival. The Indians were so awe-struck by the smoke-belching behemoths that they sometimes accompanied them along the shore for miles.

A top-hatted half-breed trader warily sits on his freshly un-loaded stock, while an interpreter delivers his salesman's spiel to a band of potential customers. The tribesmen bar-tered furs, buffalo robes and moccasins for merchandise rang-ing from flour and bed ticking to buckshot and tobacco.

July Fourth celebrants enjoy sunshine and ice cream while strolling aboard the garlanded *Newella* at Leavenworth, Kansas, in the 1860s.

5 | Good times, bad times

The tempo of life along the Missouri was irresistibly linked to the moods of what newspaperman-humorist George Fitch once described as "a river that plays hide-and-seek with you today, and tomorrow follows you around like a pet dog with a dynamite cracker tied to its tail."

Residents looked to the river for essential sustenance, including a limitless quantity of cloudy but wholesome drinking water and an abundant supply of tasty catfish, dubbed by one fancier as "this best of all fishes." And every spring, the arrival of the season's first steamboat bearing produce and supplies touched off a celebration rivaled on the calendar only by the Fourth of July.

The capricious river brought prosperity to some towns and disaster to others. A well-located steamboat center like Yankton, Dakota Territory, in the 1870s, provided the zesty spectacle of roustabouts, bullwhackers, prospectors, land speculators and homesteaders rubbing elbows in the town's four hotels, 73 stores, 30 saloons and one ice-cream parlor. Yankton also boasted a college, an insane asylum and a double-edged reputation. Residents saw no inconsistency in acknowledging that it was "one of the worst of the river towns" for its wide-open ways, while also praising "the tone, refinement and culture pervading its society."

Many locations were not so fortunate. A record 41-foot flood in 1881 wiped out Green Island, Nebraska; and Brunswick, Missouri, found itself a mile inland after the river abruptly changed course in 1875. As for Carroll, Montana, which once hoped to rival bustling Fort Benton, an itinerant grocer wrote its epitaph in 1874. Stuck on a stranded steamboat, he lamented that the only potential customers for miles around were in Carroll "and they haven't got a hundred dollars all told."

Completing a Missouri crossing, local residents and their
horses wait for the ferryman to secure his rope-drawn craft
at Wilder's Landing, Montana Territory. Such ferries did
a brisk business, charging tolls that ranged from a dime for
a pedestrian to 75 cents for a loaded wagon and team.

162

The inevitable saloon, with the owner's wife standing demurely beside the doorway, beckons from the riverbank at Rocky Point, Montana. The saloon, which doubled as a restaurant, was one of a dozen rude buildings clustered at the site of a popular ferry crossing below Fort Benton.

A bustling hotel in Bismarck, Dakota Territory, shows off
its guests, staff and station wagon while roofers work on un-
concernedly. Named for the famed Iron Chancellor in the
hope of attracting German investors, Bismarck was known
for years by its homely original name: The Crossing.

A first-class ticket in the 1870s from Helena, Montana Territory, to Chicago covered the stage to Fort Benton, boat to Bismarck (misspelled), and rail to Sauk Rapids, St. Paul and Chicago. Fare: $71.

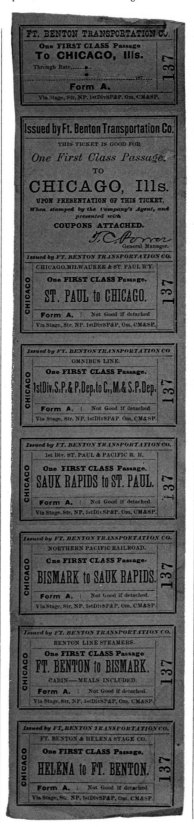

D. McEachran, who passed through in 1881 on his way to Fort Benton.

"Bismarck," he wrote, "was started by the opening of a whiskey shop and though it now contains a population of over 2,000, the example set by the pioneer has been faithfully followed, since at least three-fourths of the buildings are grog shops, gambling houses or places of amusement. Having three days to wait for our steamer we took advantage of a high Government functionary's offer to show us the 'city by gaslight.'

"Our first visit was to a 'keno' house where we stayed but a short time for the disgusting sight of gambling in its worst form, and the foul air and still fouler language drove us away. We next visited a faro bank where similar scenes presented themselves. We could not help remarking on the general expression of abandonment depicted in the faces and nervous expressions of the frequenters of these dens.

"Our next place of visit was to the 'opera house,' a wooden structure, the entrance of which is a barroom. At the counter tickets had to be procured, the charge for entrance to the ground floor being twenty five cents, to the boxes fifty cents. We looked into the pit. Here we saw a sawdust covered floor, rough, unplaned board seats and forty or fifty frontiersmen, all with large, wide brimmed hats and nearly all smoking or chewing tobacco.

"Ascending the narrow stairway we reached the gallery which was partitioned into curtained boxes—which are connected to the stage and in which actresses spend their time between the acts being regaled by beer or champagne according to the extravagance of the occupants. About half a dozen women acted as waiters and their dress

and manners indicated the life of immorality which they lead. The scenery on stage was of the most primitive nature and the acting was execrable. While we were looking on, a large woman with a voice like a cow horn attempted a vulgar ditty, 'Champagne and Oysters.'"

The attitudes that so startled McEachran in Bismarck's dens sometimes spilled over into more august premises. In one such case in 1873, merchants and civic leaders called for a meeting in the courthouse at Yankton to discuss a bond sale proposed by directors of the Dakota Southern Railroad. Liberals and Democrats (known as the Broadway Gang) opposed the idea while Republicans (the Capitol Street Gang) supported it vehemently. General Edwin Stanton McCook, a huge ex-Civil War officer, then serving as the territorial governor's secretary, had supported the sale for weeks—but not without bitter objection from a leading member of the opposition, banker Peter Wintermute. The two men nodded politely when they encountered each other before the meeting in the bar of the St. Charles Hotel, which stood next door to the courthouse. But when Wintermute discovered that he was out of cigars and asked the other man to loan him one, the general turned him down; and then, after an argument, beat him up.

General McCook was a man of robust instincts—the Dakota *Herald* regarded him as an "ignorant, vainglorious, drunken lout, who is an eyesore to our people and a depression upon the good morals of this community." Peter Wintermute weighed only 135 pounds, and the general proceeded, according to later testimony, to push the banker's head into a cuspidor. The vic-

A stern-wheeler rests on wooden ways at Bismarck in 1886. Boats were winched up by steam engine allowing workmen to repair hulls, rudders and steering mechanisms. In winter, as many as five steamers could be hoisted and stored side by side, safe from the Missouri's crushing ice.

191

tim cleaned himself up and went to the meeting anyhow —but with a pistol, which he used to shoot his tormentor as soon as he saw him again. The big man charged once more—though this time with blood dripping down his coat front—seized the little banker, who was still firing, and tried to throw him through a window. But the general was mortally wounded and died on the following morning.

A jury eventually found Wintermute innocent of manslaughter, but he died of tuberculosis caught in the dank cell that he inhabited while awaiting trial. News of the deaths was received by the men's colleagues with grave headwagging; incidents of similar violence by roustabouts caused little stir, but prosperity was producing men of property—with wives who harbored social ambitions—and, thus, an awareness of class that had not existed a decade before.

Yankton's leading lights boasted in the mid-1870s that the population included 90 college graduates, and applauded a high-toned female visitor who opined: "The tone and refinement and culture pervading Yankton's society might at first incline a traveler from the East to suppose he had been moving in a circuit which had brought him to the point from which he had started rather than in the wilds of a territory."

The lust for culture and refinement engendered absurd strictures on occasion. In 1876 the territorial legislature passed a statute, universally ignored, which prohibited Sunday buggy riding save by those on their way to church, to a doctor's office or to a funeral. But solid citizens laid a stratum of respectability over the yeastier impulses of Yankton for all that—as did solid citizens in other steamboat towns—and dominated the affairs of the upper river as they did so.

Ladies were conscious of style; they had their pick of silks, prints and various furs at the local dry goods stores. Hostesses did not lack for fancy groceries—almonds, lemon syrup in cans, oysters in glass jars and brandied cherries. Young men of promise matched wits at weekly meetings of the Literary and Debating Club. But they were also privy to social intercourse with the fair sex at spelling bees, dances on the decks of steamboats that were docked at the levee, and group excursions through the countryside around the town to hunt wild fruit for canning. Lecturers were prized: frontier ladies applauded loudly when suffragette Susan B.

Anthony urged them into the battle for women's rights.

But it took even more glamorous visitors to Yankton —Lieutenant Colonel George Armstrong Custer, his wife, Elizabeth, and officers of the 7th U.S. Cavalry —to prompt the steamboat era's supreme social occasion; the one that was envied by other river towns and that served as a kind of catalyst by which those who were safely embosomed in polite society and those who were simply scrabbling about on its fringes were sorted out for good and all.

The 7th came into Yankton by rail on April 9, 1873, bound for its historic and tragic service on the frontier, and camped under canvas near Rhine Creek on the outskirts of town. Local merchants were pleased. Custer had 800 officers and enlisted men in his command, plus 700 horses, 200 mules and 40 laundresses. Joseph R. Hanson and C. H. McIntyre contracted to supply 300 tons of hay and James M. Stone to deliver 300 cords of wood; a vanguard of officer's wives took rooms in hotels, and Mrs. Custer rented a small house in town and moved into it with her servants, Mary and Ham. But Yanktonians were thrown into a more intimate and difficult relationship with the visiting cavalrymen a week later.

A cold rain began spattering the area. Soon the rain turned to dry snow, the wind rose, the temperature fell alarmingly, and both town and camp were engulfed by a blinding spring blizzard. The storm lasted for 36 hours; tents blew down, the snow piled into deep drifts and troopers began staggering through the white gloom toward town leading horses in dire need of shelter. Others sought cover for themselves. Mrs. Custer opened her door to a half dozen of them and rolled them up in carpets to restore warmth to their bodies. But this time civilians came to the rescue of the cavalry. Barns, livery stables and warehouses were reopened to the regiment's horses and mules; and parties of muffled townsmen succored shivering soldiers and frightened laundresses—one of whom had just given birth to a baby.

Yankton experienced a heady sense of possessiveness in the process of delivering the soldiers from the elements. Custer was not just any colonel (the town referred to him by his grander Civil War title: Brevet Major General); and the very word *cavalry* suggested an élan, a certain steely chic, that infantry simply could not match. The snow had barely begun to thaw before

the best people were jostling each other to plan and prepare a celebration by which the 7th and its gaudy commander could be formally welcomed into their hearts —and by which those citizens who received invitations could bask, modestly, in the reflected glamor and cozy sense of exclusivity the event was certain to provide.

The proceedings were duly reported by the Yankton *Press,* issue of April 30:

"The social event of 1873 occurred in Yankton on Thursday evening last on the occasion of the Reception Ball given by the citizens of Yankton to the officers of the 7th Cavalry.

"The Reception Ball was held at Stone's Hall, which was profusely decorated with Flags, the walls being completely hid from view by starry banners arranged in the most attractive and tasteful manner, while the ceiling was hung with like emblems gracefully festooned. These striking ornaments with the bright full-dress uniforms of the military gentlemen present was sufficient to call to mind Byron's famous 'Battle of Waterloo.' There were present about 120 couples embracing the leading commercial men of Yankton with

their ladies; while the officers were fully represented.

"The Seventh Cavalry band led by our former townsman Felix Vinatieri, furnished the music which could not have been better. Vinatieri also added much interest to the entertainment by his wonderful skill as a violinist, in rendering the 'mocking bird.'

" 'Rosy Morn' peeped through the windows before the company thought of separating, and when the 'adieu and safe return' signalled the closing of the Reception Ball the parting was most reluctant."

It was a far more symbolic occasion than the Yankton *Press* could have imagined. The "leading commercial men" of the river ports wanted to obtain white control of the wilderness upriver; they wanted the anarchic Sioux contained in reservations at last—and living off government bounty that would be shipped from warehouses along their levees. George Custer and his cavalrymen paid for the Reception Ball on the Little Bighorn; they were human sacrifices who forced the Army into final containment of the wild tribes, and ensured that future upon which speculators had so rashly gambled after gaining the riverbank from Strike-the-Ree.

A few embellishments to lure commerce

By the late 1860s, when steamboat ports were booming on the upper Missouri, the older towns on the lower river had begun to settle into a comfortable municipal middle age. Their chambers of commerce often sought to show off their hard-won respectability by means of a visual device dear to the hearts of western promoters: the panoramic map, a bird's-eye view created by a skilled —and highly imaginative—artist.

While impressively accurate in many details, the panoramas ofttimes indulged in flights of self-serving fancy: steamboats lined levees that had long fallen into disuse; trains sped along nonexistent railbeds and bridges; and smoke belched industriously from vacant factories. The deliberate deceptions, designed to attract new residents and industry, were studiously ignored by the townspeople who prominently displayed the maps on the walls of their homes and offices.

Especially prized were the handsome maps painstakingly crafted by Albert Ruger, a German-born artist who produced no fewer than 198 such panoramas during the course of a long and prolific career. Ruger would sometimes spend weeks walking the streets of a town, sketching every building and landmark. The result, as seen in each of the three maps of old river towns that are reproduced here and on the following pages, was a remarkably detailed vista in which all streets, churches, schools and other noteworthy structures were labeled, and where the pleasing aura of commercial vitality was always present, whether it existed or not.

The oldest white settlement on the Missouri River, St. Charles was 100 years old when this

BIRD'S EYE VIEW OF THE CITY OF

T CHARLES

ST. CHARLES CO.

MISSOURI 1869.

CHURCHES:
8 EVANGELICAL
9 LUTHERAN
10 METHODIST
11 GERMAN METHODIST
12 PRESBYTERIAN
13 R. CATHOLIC
14 CONVENT OF THE SACRED HEART

COURT HOUSE

panorama appeared in 1869. But the railroad bridge, one of the longest of its type in the country, was not completed until two years later.

MISSOURI RIVER

DRAWN BY A. RUGER.

1. COURT HOUSE.
2. COUNTY JAIL.
3. PUBLIC SCHOOL.
4. MASONIC COLLEGE.
5. BAPTIST SEMINARY.
6. PRESBYTERIAN SEMINARY.
7. ARCANA HALL, TURNER HALL.
8. MARKET HOUSE.
9. L & ST. JOE. R.W. DEPOT.

COURT HOUSE.

BIRD'S

LEX

LAFA

196   Once prosperous Lexington—where the *Saluda* exploded in 1852, killing more than 100 Mormons—had fallen on hard times by

1869, despite the illusion given of a busy river port. The walled area at left is the campus of the world's first Masonic college.

197

REFERENCES
1 Court House
2 Public School
3 Midland Pacific
 R. R. Depot
4 Steamboat Landing
5 Cemetary.

NEBRA

OTOE COUNT

BIRD'S EY

At one time a booming jump-off point for overland freight wagons bound for the West, Nebraska City had begun by 1868 to pin

CITY.

PAWNEE ST.

SIOUX ST.

CHURCHES
6 Episcopal
7 Baptist
8 Catholic
9 ?
10 German Methodist
11 South
12 Old School
13 United
14 Cumberland
15 Christian
16 Lutheran

its future hopes on the railroad. But the tracks seen curving into town at the top of the map did not actually arrive until 1871.

6 | In service to the Army

General Alfred Sully, who employed 15 steamboats to transport troops and supplies while campaigning against the Sioux on the upper Missouri in the early 1860s, later wrote that the "conquest of the Missouri Valley would have been a very different matter had the government been deprived of this important aid in its operations."

The steamboat's role in the service of the Indian-fighting Army was as varied as it was indispensable. Throughout this long and bloody struggle it was the main carrier of supplies to well-established military posts along the upper river as well as to isolated depots, where it left food, ammunition and other provisions for troops on the march.

The steamboat was also invaluable strategically; it was not only the fastest way to move soldiers upstream or down, to points where they were needed in a hurry, but it also maintained communications between units separated by a stretch of river too wide, deep and fast to be forded by mounted messengers. In addition, the steamer was frequently pressed into service as reconnaissance vessel, floating hospital and—armed with howitzers as well as riflemen—powerful gunboat.

Besides being a principal factor in the Army's ultimate victory over the Indians, the steamboat served heroically at the time of the Army's most devastating defeat at the hands of the hostiles. In a harrowing race downstream after the debacle at the Little Bighorn, *Far West,* Custer's supporting supply boat, carried to safety wounded survivors of the battle that cost the lives of Custer and his entire column of troops.

A steamer unloads military supplies at Cow Island in 1880 at a broad bend of the Missouri. The soldiers *(foreground)*, belong to the encamped detachment guarding equipment stockpiled at the wilderness depot.

Riot abouts an the far west

Steaming "from a field of havoc to a station of mourners"

Men blunder into history so myopically that they are seldom aware, until they find themselves involved in some enormous drama, of being cast and costumed by the fates. The 7th U.S. Cavalry was immersed in its own mundane exasperations as it rode out of Dakota Territory's Fort Abraham Lincoln on May 17, 1876, to engage in climactic battle with the Sioux. Nothing in the unit's experience of Indian warfare portended the mass of mounted warriors Chief Crazy Horse was mobilizing along the remote streams that fed the Yellowstone. No trooper — and, indeed, no general of the Western Command — could imagine that George Armstrong Custer would soon plunge the regiment into suicidal defeat, allow the Indians to demean the Army before the world and, in so doing, launch Captain Grant Marsh on the wildest, fastest steamboat voyage in American history.

Forty per cent of the 7th's troopers were raw recruits who had been brought in to replace "snowbirds" —men who had joined up to keep warm during the winter but who had deserted with the advent of spring. Its enlisted men had been driven hard, in consequence, and — worse yet — had been denied pay for two months at Fort Lincoln to prevent their drinking whiskey "to the further loss and detriment of discipline." They were not amused to discover that an Army paymaster was accompanying them during the first day's march, and was waiting to disburse the overdue cash as soon as they dismounted at their first temptationless bivouac. They had no means, furthermore, of grasping the full irony of this niggardly delay: a good deal of the money was to find

its way into a war fund maintained by Crazy Horse after his Sioux warriors collected it from the pockets of dead cavalrymen on the Little Bighorn.

Captain Marsh had arrived at Fort Lincoln 10 days after the regiment rode out. He tied up at the bank and loaded oats, bran, medical supplies, tents, tarpaulins and small-arms ammunition on which the 7th was to draw during its excursion into the wilds. General Phil Sheridan had asked Marsh to fulfill a special assignment: as master and pilot, to select the one steamer that could be expected — as Army supply boat, hospital ship, mobile command post and instrument of quick river crossings — to stay closest to the action during the summer's campaign. Marsh felt well prepared. No pilot in America understood the Yellowstone as well as he. No vessel, he felt, was better suited for it than the stern-wheeler *Far West,* a 190-foot upper-river boat he had picked, on being given his choice, from all the steamers operated by the Coulson Packet Company. But if Marsh was ready for the Rockies and the Sioux, he had given no thought at all to a more subtle but no less daunting adversary: George Custer's pretty wife, Libbie.

Knots of officers' wives approached the riverbank almost as soon as Marsh put his boat against the shore to begin loading. He asked them aboard, instructed his steward to give them as "dainty" a lunch as could be managed, excused himself, and went back to work. He was interrupted at noon; Mrs. Custer and the ladies, the steward informed him, would be desolated if the captain did not preside at the luncheon table. Marsh was busy; proper loading was crucial to a vessel bound for shallow water. But he broke off, went to his quarters to make himself presentable, and joined the women in *Far West*'s little cabin. Mrs. Custer seated herself on his right, and put Mrs. Algernon E. Smith, wife of one of her husband's lieutenants, on Marsh's left. Marsh began to enjoy himself; both women regarded him with ob-

---

Among the images sketched in pencil by artist William Cary during an 1874 voyage on *Far West* were these roustabouts and a heavy-caliber, lever-action carbine used by one of the boat's meat hunters.

vious admiration. He did not realize that he was a target of female machination until he rose to excuse himself at the end of the meal. The Mesdames Custer and Smith rose with him, drew him aside and offered him a dismaying confidence: they were going with him to join the 7th, if—and the demeanor of the colonel's lady suggested that this was a foregone conclusion—Captain Marsh was willing to take them.

Marsh had chosen *Far West* for the summer campaign because she would draw only 30 inches of water with the cargo he was presently loading; moreover, her minimal upper works and two powerful engines made her wonderfully handy in high winds. But he had wanted as few free riders as possible, too; *Far West* would accommodate no more than 30 cabin passengers. He indicated her cramped and spartan quarters with a wave of the hand; he was certain the ladies had not considered the danger and discomfort their request would involve. Mrs. Custer smiled patiently. Her husband had *authorized* her to join him, she said, *and* by traveling on this very boat. Marsh had no reason to doubt her. She had joined Custer on hair-brained excursions before. But—Custer or not—Marsh would not have them on his boat. He went on, with real embarrassment, to express regret. The ladies let him stammer a bit before turning, stiffly, to go ashore.

He put this awkwardness behind him the next morning. His deck hands cast off *Far West's* lines; Marsh pulled her whistle cord and headed her upstream toward less disconcerting conflict. The boat had a good crew: two dependable engineers in George Foulk and John Hardy, a fine second pilot in Dave Campbell, and a deck and fireroom force of 30 hardy men. She took aboard a military guard—60 riflemen of the 6th Infantry —during a layover at Ford Buford. She also picked up Brigadier General Alfred H. Terry, whom she was to serve as a kind of landlocked flagship, and took him upstream to meet Colonel John Gibbon and a force of infantry that Gibbon was leading down river. A bracing sense of anticipation seized all aboard.

The Missouri River runs roughly east and west and, thus, roughly parallel to the Canadian border as it crosses western North Dakota and eastern Montana. The Yellowstone River enters the Big Muddy from the southwest at an angle of about 45 degrees near the bor-

Eight members of Fort Berthold's 70-man garrison meet in front of the commanding officer's quarters in 1865. Taken over from the American Fur Company in 1864, the ramshackle post was famed for an inexhaustible supply of whiskey delivered by steamer before it was deserted in 1867.

Custer was given liberty by Terry to ignore these strictures if he "saw sufficient reason for departing from them." Gibbon did not leave it quite at that. "Now don't be greedy, Custer," he said, as the council broke up. "There are Indians enough for all. Wait for us."

Custer's tent had been erected on the bank only a few yards from the boat. He hurried ashore and began issuing orders to men who materialized out of the darkness. One of Gibbon's lieutenants, watching from the deck, guessed — as he wrote in his journal — that the infantry "had little hope of being in at the death. . . . Custer will undoubtedly exert himself to the utmost to win all the laurels." The horse soldiers themselves quickly came to the same conclusion. Custer had been urged to take three Gatling guns with his column, and Gibbon had offered to lend him four extra troops of cavalry. He had refused these encumbrances. He expected a long chase, and he now ordered his pack animals loaded with extra forage as well as 15 days' rations and 50 rounds of reserve ammunition for every trooper. He responded irritably when his commanders suggested that Reno's mules, worn out by their long scouting trip, would break down under such loads: "Well, gentlemen," he said, "you may carry what supplies you please, but you will be held responsible. We will follow until we catch them. You had better take extra salt; we may have to live on horse meat."

It was not a night for sleep aboard *Far West;* Grant Marsh was enmeshed in George Custer's compulsion for surrounding himself with members of his immediate family. A brother, Captain Thomas Custer, and the commander's brother-in-law, Lieutenant James Calhoun, were among the officers of the 7th. Custer had also managed to mount two civilian relatives in his wilderness cavalcade: his 17-year-old nephew Henry Armstrong ("Autie") Reed and his light-hearted youngest brother, Boston Custer.

Tom Custer and James Calhoun were among a restless throng of scouts, staff officers and cavalry commanders who drifted into *Far West's* cabin after midnight; they soon involved themselves — and Marsh — in a high-stakes poker game. Marsh was startled at the feckless betting that ensued. Rescued by duty, he went to unload *Far West's* stores before sunrise. But the cavalrymen left thousands of dollars in a heap on the table at dawn; an infantry captain, W. H. H. Crom-

The famed *Far West*, gangplank poised and firewood stacked, prepares to load freight for an upriver run. Chartered by the Army in 1876 for $360 a day, she served gallantly with the ill-fated Custer expedition and later carried the peace commissioners who treated with the Sioux.

and channel catfish hung in the clear water that streamed over the Bighorn's gravel bottom and after a while Marsh, Engineer Foulk, Pilot Campbell and Captain Baker left the boat to try their luck as well. Foulk found himself staring at the willow thickets that bordered the stream's eastern bank; an Indian, he said—if any Indians were left to try—would have no trouble taking cover there to fire at the lot of them.

A naked, mounted tribesman burst instantly through the screen of bushes at which they were looking, jerked his lathered pony to a halt at the water's edge, and held up a carbine in the peace sign. They saw with relief that he wore the erect Crow scalp lock; and they recognized him, a few seconds later, as Curley, a scout who had ridden with Custer. They waved him forward and hurried toward the steamer as he pushed his horse across the stream. But Curley simply sank to his knees, once aboard the boat, and began rocking from side to side and bellowing as if in agony. Baker eventually produced a pencil and a piece of paper, demonstrated their use, and handed them to him. He threw himself flat on the deck, gripped the pencil in one fist, and drew a careful circle. He made a larger circle outside it and began jabbing dots into the space between them. "Sioux," he cried. "Sioux, Sioux, Sioux!" He twisted up to stare at them, and then, making dots within the inner circle, began yelling: "Absaroka! Absaroka!"

"By Scotts," said Marsh. "I know what *that* means. It means soldiers. That Englishman, Courtney, who runs the woodyard at the head of Drowned Man's Rapids told me so. Some Crows were there one time and he told me they were going to Camp Cooke to see the Absaroka." Absaroka was, in fact, the word—meaning The People—by which Crows defined themselves, but which, because they admired the Army for shooting up Sioux, Blackfeet and others of their ancient enemies, they generously used to describe U.S. soldiers as well.

"Absaroka!" cried Curley, leaping to his feet on hearing Marsh use the word. He poked his fingers at his chest and yelled: "Poof! Poof! Poof Absaroka!"

Baker was the first to understand the import of this pantomime. "We're whipped," he said. "That's what's the matter." The news seemed worse as they laboriously interviewed the Indian in sign language. He told them that he had escaped the battlefield on the Little Bighorn by pulling a blanket over his head (it was later

212

Officers and wives promenade while troopers crowd lower decks of two transports in the 1880s. Normally, a Missouri steamer would carry some 200 men. The photo, previously unpublished and printed from a damaged plate, was taken by Captain John Pitman, Fort Lincoln's ordnance officer.

Carrying survivors from the Little Bighorn,
Grant Marsh in *Far West* raced 700 miles
in 54 hours. "As fast as a railroad train
in a narrow, winding stream," is how St.
Paul's *Pioneer Press* described the feat.

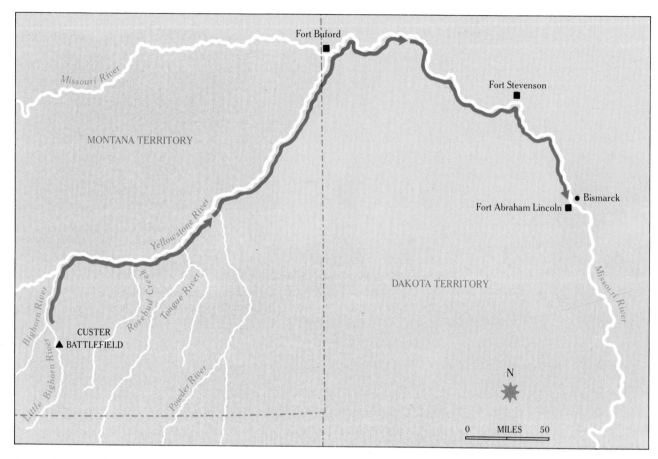

learned that he had actually run away before the fight-
ing really began) and he seemed to believe that the entire regiment had been annihilated.

Far West's crew spent an uneasy night, and its
trigger-happy sentries greeted one "Muggins" Taylor, a
scout from Gibbon's column, with a wild fusillade when
he rode up to the boat before dawn. Taylor was reeling
with exhaustion after surviving a long, desperate chase
by Sioux horsemen during the night. But he knew what
had happened to the 7th: that Custer had violated the
Western Command's best-laid plan of campaign and
had attacked without waiting for Terry.

Taylor reported that Custer had divided his forces
into three detachments and had died with one of them
—five companies of cavalrymen he led in person. Also
killed were Autie, Boss, Tom, Calhoun and Mark Kellogg—a reporter for the *Bismarck Tribune*. Elements of
the other seven companies, under Major Reno and Captain Frederick Benteen, had survived 36 hours of fight-
ing—though with many casualties—and the Indians had

finally pulled away. Though finding some relief in learning they were not about to be attacked, *Far West*'s
crew soon received orders from Terry that gave them
pause. Gibbon's infantry had found 59 wounded horse
soldiers, of whom 52 were still alive; the steamer was
to take these survivors—and news of the catastrophe
—to Fort Abraham Lincoln with all possible dispatch.

Chilling words: Marsh could only wonder how he
would be remembered if further harm came to men
wounded in so tragic a battle. He prepared to receive
the casualties by setting crew and military guard to cutting wild grass that grew luxuriantly in marshy patches
along the river. They piled it 18 inches deep on open
deck space aft of the boilers and stretched tarpaulins
across it to create a vast, soft communal mattress. Medicine chests were hauled up from the steamer's hold.
But exasperating—and pathetic—misadventures delayed delivery of the wounded men.

Pack mules grew unruly at the battlefield when they
were harnessed to stretchers made of abandoned Sioux

lodge poles. They tossed their helpless freight. Soldiers of Gibbon's force finally tried carrying the wounded down the Little Bighorn valley on hand-litters; but gave up at midnight — utterly exhausted — after covering less than five miles. The hapless survivors lay in the open the next day while more tractable mules were rounded up and new stretchers constructed. It was sundown before the caravan of invalids — each hoisted between two animals and guarded by four men — once more began its slow way down the valley. Then it rained. The procession was halted once more — this time by boggy land and pitch darkness — at midnight.

Marsh now intervened. He turned out his crew and set them to building bonfires along the three miles of river bottom that separated the stretcher column from its goal. The long line of mules and men emerged in firelight around the steamer at two in the morning; and crew, guard and attendant soldiers carried the wounded to the boat's makeshift hospital. With them came a haggard, bewhiskered Army physician, Dr. Henry R. Porter, who must, in retrospect, be considered the truest hero of the Battle of the Little Bighorn.

Porter had lived, though only by miracles, to be the only survivor of the 7th's three regimental surgeons; man after man had been hit and killed within inches of him. He had maintained a sardonic coolness when Major Reno led his men in a wild stampede to the barren knoll upon which they made their stand; and — having stayed behind with a dying soldier, and having ridden alone through a storm of Sioux fire to rejoin them — had walked among the wounded there as if oblivious of the arrows and bullets that hit one in three of all around him. Now, after wringing Marsh's hand, he looked to the wounded once again before surrendering to sleep in one of *Far West's* cabins.

One more refugee of battle was now led up to the steamer: a lurching, wounded sorrel stallion named Comanche; the beast had been ridden to Custer's fight by Captain Myles Keogh and was the only living creature to have survived it. Marsh took the horse aboard, ordered a grass-padded stall built for him aft, and — sorting through some of Gibbon's people who had followed the wounded down the valley — found a hysterical veterinary surgeon and hauled him aboard, too. "He was," the pilot said later, "the worst scared man I ever saw — the terror of Indians had entered his soul." Marsh bul-

lied him into dressing the horse's wounds. Comanche, thus attended, lived to become a symbol of heroism for the 7th, and was led — bridled, saddled, but riderless and draped in black — in all regimental parades until he died peacefully at the age of 28.

Successful steamboat pilots, and particularly those who lasted on the upper Missouri, seem to have been buoyed by some blend of optimism, self-confidence and serenity. Marsh was no exception. But he found himself, with the approach of sunrise, falling prey to a weakening sense of uncertainty — compounded from the sight of the wounded on his deck, from the realization of tragedy that was growing on all around him, and from a hard, professional understanding of the kind of water he would have to run before reaching the Missouri. It was not dissipated when General Terry rode up at dawn, disheveled and depressed, to rejoin the vessel.

Terry, a Connecticut lawyer who had become a professional soldier after service in the Civil War, was not a man for dramatics, but he called Marsh to his cabin after coming aboard and spoke with surprising emotion: "Captain, this is a bad river. You have the most precious cargo a boat ever carried. Every soldier here is the victim of a terrible blunder. A sad and terrible blunder. I wish to ask you to use all the skill you possess."

"I will give you my best," said Marsh. But his nerve failed him after he climbed to the pilothouse. *Far West* had to be turned from one narrow channel into another around the island against which she was moored, and had then to be headed into fast water downstream. The pilot — "I felt sick" — could not imagine bringing it off, although he had handled boats in hundreds of similar situations without a moment of conscious thought. Campbell, the second pilot, and the mate, Ben Thompson, had seated themselves on the bench at the rear of the wheelhouse. "Boys," Marsh said, turning to them, "I can't do it. I'll smash her up."

"Oh, no you won't," said Campbell. "Cool off a minute and you'll be all right."

Marsh leaned against the wheel and stared silently ahead. He ordered the steamer's lines to be cast off after a bit, rang up the engine room, turned the island — and began reacting, in a daze of concentration, to the kaleidoscopic succession of chutes, islands, rocks and rapids that were flung across his field of vision by the boat's startling speed in the narrow waterway. ◉

The 178-foot *Josephine*, a Missouri stern-wheeler converted for river-improvement work, dwarfs *Baby Josephine* beside her. The smaller boat

The chore of taming "Old Misery"

Engineers' insigne, dating from 1839, symbolizes early forts.

In the 1870s, as intensifying Indian warfare in the region of the upper Missouri made dependable delivery of Army supplies by steamboat more imperative than ever, the federal government finally felt compelled to reduce the river's perils to navigation.

The job of improving "Old Misery" —as it was ruefully known—was entrusted mainly to the Army's Corps of Engineers. The steamboats themselves played an important role, often serving as working platforms for labor crews, who either lived aboard when onshore accommodations were not available or in barracks-like scows that were towed behind the steamers.

The improvement program consisted not only of clearing the streambed of dead trees and other obstructions but also of altering sections of the river itself. Surveys conducted by the Corps of Engineers pinpointed the specific danger spots, among them rapids on the upper river through which safe passageways had to be blasted and stretches where bank erosion, especially in the flood season, sometimes choked steamboat channels with sediment overnight. (The clogging of the Missouri at Sioux

used in water too shallow for her companion.

City was so bad in 1879 that wags told the story of a woman who attempted to commit suicide by jumping into the river, only to find herself stuck in two feet of mud.)

The Engineers relied on a number of techniques to keep the river open and to check bank erosion. One of the most effective was the building of "training structures"—dikes and piers angled into the river to divert the current away from an eroding shore line. These structures also increased the river's velocity, thus loosening sediment on the bottom and deepening the channel for steamboats.

A U.S. Engineers surveyor takes bearings on the Missouri around 1889.

Crews surveying a stretch of the Missouri near Fort Benton line up aboard their living quarters: canvas-roofed barges called quarterboats.

Entitled by rank to the best quarters, officers of the Corps of Engineers relax with their wives in *Josephine*'s spacious aftercabin.

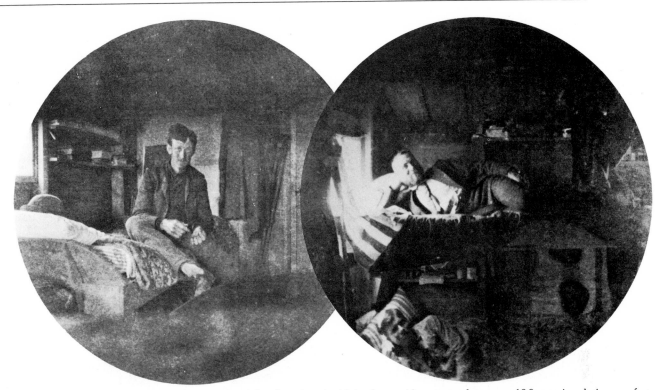

Large quarterboats, floating barracks made of wood and equipped with bunks, could accommodate up to 100 men in relative comfort.

Maneuvering in shallow water close to the Missouri shore, *Baby Josephine* throws up a fine spray with her pint-sized paddle wheel.

Near a railroad bridge at Omaha in 1880, U.S. Engineers, supplied by steamboat, supervise the weaving of a huge retainer made of saplings and

designed to arrest cave-ins along the bank. Boulders anchored it in place.

It was axiomatic among pilots that every river had to be "learned" twice—going up and going down. Neither Marsh nor any other steamboatman had ever seen the Bighorn going down, and his every movement of the wheel—once he had cleared the first island—stemmed from split-second decisions that were based on instinct alone. It was sometimes possible, on larger streams, to briefly offset fast water by running paddle wheels in reverse; but the restricted Bighorn refused a pilot time for such a maneuver and, since a boat could not maintain steerageway without moving faster than the water going past her rudders, *Far West's* hurtling descent of rapids was almost more, at times, than her passengers could bear to watch.

Marsh covered 53 miles before the afternoon was spent, and tied up below the river's bank. Pilots and crew now found themselves immersed in anticlimax. Fourteen of *Far West's* wounded had recovered enough to be moved ashore. All but one of the rest—a man who shortly died—seemed to have passed the point of real danger. General Terry disembarked to make his headquarters at a riverside Army depot. He decided, though reluctantly, to hold the vessel there for two days in order to ferry Gibbon's weary infantrymen, now marching back from the battlefield, to sure safety on the north bank of the Yellowstone.

Western history has not, because of this pause, included Marsh's run down the Bighorn in the overall mileage that was covered in *Far West's* subsequent and astonishing race to Fort Lincoln. It is doubtful, nevertheless, that any other pilot ever covered such water at such speed. It is hard not to think, too—since men gain in élan from winning against odds—that Marsh, Campbell and the vessel's two engineers drove her more recklessly, once underway again, than might have been possible had they not discovered reserves of cunning and determination in themselves during the first, frightening hours of their voyage.

The Yellowstone was wider and less precipitous than the Bighorn, and *Far West's* crew had come to know it well. But it was a difficult, dangerous and reef-littered river, nevertheless; and Marsh—who was proud of his reputation as a pilot, proud of the responsibility with which the Army had entrusted him, and invigorated by the dramatic role in which he found himself—lengthened the odds that every steamer normally faced

221

Sioux Indians, with a few whites, crowd the upper decks of the Power Line packet *Helena* en route to the Indian agency at Standing Rock, below Bismarck, around 1880. Crushing Army pressure was forcing the Sioux onto reservations, though a number held out in Canada until 1881.

in negotiating it by resolving to run his vessel day and night until he reached Fort Lincoln and to crack on every possible pound of steam while doing so.

They set off at 5 p.m. on June 30. Sunlight lingered late, the sky stayed providentially clear, and dawn came early as *Far West* plunged downstream, with Marsh and Campbell standing alternate four-hour tricks at the wheel. But those who stared into the gloom as the boat swung through bends and down stretches of fast water found the short summer night the longest of their lives. An exhilarating excitement grew aboard the boat, for all that, as she churned on into the dazzling sunlight of morning—an excitement that was reflected (and more accurately, perhaps, than the 20th Century mind would guess) in the lurid prose *Far West* continued to inspire long after her trip was done.

"It was a strange land and an unknown river," wrote a correspondent for the St. Paul *Pioneer Press* in an article entitled: *A Lightning Steamboat Ride.* "She was running from a field of havoc to a station of mourners. What a cargo on that steamer! What news for the country! A steamboat moving as fast as a railway train in a narrow, winding stream is not a pleasure. Occasionally the bank would be touched and men would topple over like ten pins. It was a reminder of what the result would be if a snag was struck.

"*Far West* would take a shoot on this or that side of an island as the quick judgment of the pilot would dictate. Down the Yellowstone the stanch craft shot, and down that river sealed to pilots she made over twenty miles an hour. The bold captain was taking chances, but he scarcely thought of them. He was under flying orders. Lives were at stake. The engineer was instructed to keep up steam at the highest pitch. Once the gauge marked a pressure that turned his cool head and made every nerve in his powerful frame quiver. The crisis passed and *Far West* had escaped a fate more terrible than Custer's. The rate of speed was unrivaled in the annals of boating. It was a thrilling voyage!"

There was an Army depot at the mouth of the Powder. Its garrison, which had been lined up to fire a ceremonial volley (this being the Fourth of July) was dismissed as *Far West*'s whistle sounded upstream. Soldiers surged down to the bank when the steamboat tied up to take aboard personal equipment that officers of the 7th had discarded there on preparing to go into ac-

tion. Indian scouts had come downriver with odd rumors of a defeat that the depot had found outlandish; the boat's crew confirmed them, steamed on and churned, finally, into the wide Missouri.

She paused at Fort Buford and again at Fort Stevenson. At both posts excited mobs of men leaped on board clamoring for news, were given the dismaying facts and pushed ashore again as Marsh waited impatiently to start his vessel on the last lap of her race to the telegraph office at Bismarck, immediately across the river from Fort Lincoln. General Terry—not a man to abandon protocol or to forget military formality—had given Marsh careful instructions as to the dressing of his steamer for her appearance at the 7th's home post: he was to raise a flag to half-mast and to drape the boat's jackstaff and derrick in black. These things were done as the afternoon of July 5 wore on. But it was 11 o'clock at night, darkness had fallen and the wharf at Bismarck was deserted when Marsh finally rang down FINISHED WITH ENGINES.

The silent town did not stay silent long. Gangs of men from the steamer hurried noisily up the empty streets—among them Marsh, Dr. Porter, and Terry's aide-de-camp, Captain E. W. Smith, who carried a bag full of messages, dispatches for Army headquarters in Chicago, and notes that had been found beside correspondent Mark Kellogg's body on the battlefield. Lamps were lighted and householders emerged, half-dressed, at the sound of voices shouting the impossible news. Marsh, Porter and Smith routed out C. A. Lounsberry, editor of the *Bismarck Tribune,* and hurried to the telegraph office with him and with a telegrapher named J. M. Carnahan. Lounsberry was a correspondent for the New York *Herald* and after asking a few startled questions he scribbled a bulletin and handed it to Carnahan for transmission:

"Bismarck, D. T., July 6, 1876:—General Custer attacked the Indians June 25, and he with every officer and man in five companies were killed. Reno with seven companies fought in entrenched positions three days. The *Bismarck Tribune*'s special correspondent was with the expedition and was killed."

Porter, Smith and Marsh began telling their stories to Lounsberry while Carnahan transmitted the notes that Kellogg had been jotting down until the day of the fight and that General Terry personally had salvaged from the pouch beside the correspondent's body. Carnahan then dispatched a long account of the battle written by one of Gibbon's commanders. Lounsberry went on interviewing and writing; Carnahan tapped out the hand-written copy on his telegraph key.

Editor and telegrapher stayed in their chairs for 22 hours, and they made Marsh and *Far West,* as well as Porter and the 7th's officers, familiar to millions; Carnahan sent 15,000 words (telegraph tolls cost the staggering sum of $3,000) in giving the *Herald* one of the greatest stories in U.S. history. But Marsh and his vessel had one more duty. He left the telegraph office after midnight with Captain Smith, recalled his crew and crossed the river to Fort Lincoln.

Wives of the 7th's soldiers and household troops at the fort had been experiencing premonitions of disaster for two days. The fort was headquarters for a detachment of Indian police — tribesmen who served as representatives of the government — and the whites there had gradually become aware that these men were in the grip of an intense, bated excitement. "There was whispering," as one witness wrote, "and rumors of a great battle. Those who watched them knew something unusual must have happened. But what? Fleet-footed warriors mounted on fleeter animals and aided, perhaps, by signals, had brought the news. But no white man knew. It was stifling." Now, at two in the morning, the post's officers were called to headquarters, given the news by Captain Smith and, just before sunrise, asked to break it to the regiment's wives and widows.

"I have heard the women tell of their intense excitement when they heard *Far West's* whistle blast as she approached Bismarck," Edward S. Godfrey, who served with Reno, said years later, "and how they waited and waited for tidings, each afraid to tell her anxieties, til near midnight when, with heavy hearts, almost with sobs, they separated and went to their homes. My wife told me how she tossed with restlessness until dawn when she was startled from a doze by a tap on her window, and instantly exclaimed: 'Is my husband killed?' She was answered by a voice choked with emotion: 'No, dear, your husband is safe, and Mrs. Moylan's husband is safe, but all the rest are dead.' "

Lieutenant C. L. Gurley of the 6th Infantry shared a harder task. "It fell to my lot to accompany Dr. J. V. D. Middleton, our post surgeon, to the quarters of Mrs. Custer. We started on our sad errand a little before 7 o'clock on that 6th of July morning. I went to the rear of the Custer house, woke up Maria, Mrs. Custer's housemaid and requested her to rap on Mrs. Custer's door, and to say to her that she and Mrs. Calhoun and Miss Reed were wanted in the parlor. But Mrs. Custer had been awakened by the footsteps in the hall. She called me by name and asked me the cause of my early visit. I made no reply but followed Dr. Middleton into the parlor. There we were almost immediately followed by the ladies of the household and there we told to them their first intimation of the awful result of the Battle of the Little Big Horn. Imagine the grief of those stricken women, their sobs, their flood of tears."

The morning was half-gone and the sun was hot on the river before the last of *Far West's* wounded men had been taken ashore and Marsh and his officers could sit down to consider the parameters of their own accomplishments. They had come a little more than 700 miles — from the mouth of the Bighorn to Bismarck — in 54 hours. They had averaged — and this included *Far West's* stops for wood as well as her delay at the Powder River and at the two forts — 13 1/7 miles an hour over that distance. No vessel had gone that fast in all the years since Nicholas Roosevelt made his voyage to New Orleans.

But *Far West* represented something more than this ultimate triumph of steampower and human nerve. The course of history had already begun changing even as she tied up at Fort Lincoln, and both she and her crew were symbols of the past by the time their wounded soldiers had been taken ashore. The Sioux had sealed their own fate by their bloody victory over Custer. The Army was moved to extraordinary exertions in response, and within a year Indian resistance to white exploitation of the Rocky Mountain West was broken forever. The long, brave day of the Missouri's rivermen declined thereafter, for nothing now impeded railroad construction in the wilds, and the locomotive was the one predator the steamboat could not survive. *Far West's* voyage had brought an age to a stupendous climax; no American vessel ever approached her record and she remained the queen of speed when the steamboat had vanished — with her plume of smoke, her misted paddles and her mournful whistle — from the rivers of the West.

A brave alliance with the onrushing railroads

"Our great water route . . . is more than a match for the railroad, and from this day forward the importance of the Big Muddy as a commercial route will send forth its own praise by its thousands of steamers and cheap freight." This grandiose claim, voiced in the spring of 1870 in Yankton's *Union and Dakotaian* had a hollow ring and was in itself evidence that Missouri rivermen were on the defensive against the menace of the new and rapidly expanding form of transportation.

For more than a decade a state of uneasy cooperation had existed between the Missouri steamboat and the railroad, but by the 1870s this relationship was gradually turning into an all-out rivalry. Even then, so long as iron tracks merely touched the river at ports like Yankton and Bismarck, steamboaters could withstand the competition. They were still able to prosper on trade between ports and with upriver settlements not yet approached by rails. But as more and more tracks paralleled the river, the railroads drew away traffic at one port after another. With ever-increasing loss of passengers and cargo to the railroad's faster and more frequent

service, the steamers were faced with a struggle for survival.

By 1887, when the first trains puffed into Fort Benton, the northernmost river port, the battle was virtually over. But even in defeat the vessels that had played a major role in opening the West continued to perform yeoman work on the river, particularly for the government on improvement projects. And a few were still threading the winding course of the Missouri as freight and passenger packets into the early years of this century — just as they had in the steamboat's Golden Age.

226

Steamboats line up at an Omaha dock in 1865 to unload supplies used in building the first stretch of the Union Pacific Railroad.

Before the Missouri was bridged at Bismarck in 1882, steamers were a vital link for railroads, at least in warm months. Here, in 1879, freight cars are hauled from a side-wheeler used by the Northern Pacific as a ferry between railheads at Bismark and Mandan, Dakota Territory.

During the winter, with the Missouri frozen solid, steamboat ferries were of no use to the Northern Pacific. But it made no difference to the inventive railroaders: they simply laid tracks on the ice and crossed the river on their own.

Outmatched by the railroad in the late 1880s, Missouri
steamboats still managed to score an occasional triumph.
Here a train, unable to cross the river via the bridge from
Bismarck to Mandan because tracks on the far side were
flooded, surrenders its passengers to a stern-wheeler ferry.

TEXT CREDITS

For full reference on specific page credits see bibliography.

Chapter 1: Particularly useful sources for information and quotes in this chapter are: Phil E. Chappell, "A History of the Missouri River," *Transactions of the Kansas State Historical Society 1905-1906,* Vol. IX; Hiram M. Chittenden, *Early Steamboat Navigation on the Missouri River: Life and Adventures of Joseph LaBarge,* Ross & Haines, Inc., 1962; William E. Lass, *A History of Steamboating on the Upper Missouri River,* University of Nebraska Press, 1962; W. J. McDonald, "The Missouri River and Its Victims," *Missouri Historical Review,* Vol. XXI, Jan. 1927, April 1927, July 1927; John Napton, "My Trip on the Imperial in 1867," *Contributions to the Historical Society of Montana,* Vol. VIII, 1917; William J. Petersen, ed. "The Log of the Henry M. Shreve to Fort Benton in 1869," *Mississippi Valley Historical Review,* March 1945. 30—Samuel Hauser quotes from Samuel T. Hauser letters in *Samuel T. Hauser Papers,* The Beinecke Rare Book and Manuscript Library, Yale University, May 20, 1862. Chapter 2: Particularly useful sources for information and quotes: Henry M. Brackenridge, *A Journal of a Voyage up the River Missouri, Performed in 1811,* Coale & Maxwell, Pomery & Toy, 1816; Hiram Martin Chittenden, *The American Fur Trade of the Far West,* Vols. I & II, The Press of the Pioneers, 1935; Bernard De Voto, *The Course of Empire,* Houghton Mifflin, 1952; Richard Edward Oglesby, *Manuel Lisa and the Missouri Fur Trade,* University of Oklahoma Press, 1963. 70—Brackenridge description of Lisa, Douglas, pp. 400-401; 72—song, Vestal, p. 26; Lisa expresses indignation, Douglas, p. 382; 74-75—Boller quotes, Richardson, ed. Chapter 3: Particularly useful sources of information and quotes: Hiram Martin Chittenden, *Early Steamboat Navigation on the Missouri River: Life and Adventures of Joseph LaBarge,* Ross & Haines, Inc., 1962; Joseph Mills Hanson, *The Conquest of the Missouri,* Holt, Rinehart & Winston, 1946; Louis C. Hunter, *Steamboats on the Western Rivers,* Octagon Books, 1969; W. J. McDonald, "The Missouri River and Its Victims," *Missouri Historical Review,* Vol. XXI, Jan. 1927, pp. 215-232; April 1927, pp. 455-480; July 1927, pp. 581-607; John H. Morrison, *History of American Steam Navigation,* Stephen Daye Press, 1958. Chapter 4: Particularly useful sources for information and quotes: Hiram Martin Chittenden, *History of Early Steamboat Navigation on the Missouri River: Life and Adventures of Joseph LaBarge,* Ross & Haines, Inc., 1962; Joseph Mills Hanson, *The Conquest of the Missouri,* Holt, Rinehart & Winston, 1946. Chapter 5: Particularly useful sources for information and quotes: John H. Charles, "Reminiscences of John H. Charles," *Proceedings of the Academy of Science and Letters of Sioux City, Iowa for 1905-1906;* Robert F. Karolevitz, *Yankton: A Pioneer Past,* North Plains Press, 1972; Ida Mae Rees, *Sioux City as a Steamboat Port — 1856-1873,* thesis, Dept. of History, University of South Dakota, 1967; 171-172—Captain Able quote, Parker, pp. 244-251; 176-177—Koch diary extracts, Koch; 180-181, 186—Sarah Elizabeth Canfield diary extracts, pp. 190-220; 192—female visitor on Yankton, *Dakota Panorama,* p. 211. Chapter 6: Particularly useful source for information and quotes: Joseph Mills Hanson, *The Conquest of the Missouri,* Holt, Rinehart & Winston, 1946.

PICTURE CREDITS

The sources for the illustrations in this book are shown below. Credits from left to right are separated by semicolons, from top to bottom by dashes.

Cover—*Lighter Relieving a Steamboat Aground,* George Caleb Bingham, copied by John Savage, courtesy Private Collection. 2—*Missouri Roustabout at the Tiller of a Mackinaw Boat,* William Cary, copied by Oliver Willcox, courtesy The Thomas Gilcrease Institute of American History and Art, Tulsa, Oklahoma. 6,7—Courtesy Kansas State Historical Society, Topeka. 8,9—H. G. Klenze, courtesy Montana Historical Society. 10,11—Courtesy Montana Historical Society. 12,13—F. Jay Haynes, courtesy The Haynes Foundation. 14,15—Courtesy Kansas State Historical Society, Topeka. 16—Courtesy The State Historical Society of Missouri, Edwin H. Aehle Collection. 18,19—Courtesy The Walters Art Gallery. 20,21—Drawings and map by Rafael D. Palacios. 22,23—*Northern Boundary Survey Under Major Twining,* William Cary, copied by Oliver Willcox, courtesy The Thomas Gilcrease Institute of American History and Art, Tulsa, Oklahoma. 25—George Simons, courtesy Free Public Library, Council Bluffs, Iowa. 26,27—Courtesy State Historical Society of North Dakota, Bismarck, N.D. 28—Courtesy Montana Historical Society. 29—From files of Missouri Historical Society, St. Louis. 30—Sarony's, N.Y., courtesy Montana Historical Society. 33—*Missouri Deck Hands on the Fontanelle,* William Cary, copied by Oliver Willcox, courtesy The Thomas Gilcrease Institute of American History and Art, Tulsa, Oklahoma. 34, 35—H & R Studio, Inc., courtesy Paul C. Rohloff Collection, Chicago, except top far right and bottom row, courtesy Risvold Collection, Minneapolis. 36 through 39—A. E. Mathews, courtesy Montana Historical Society. 40, 41—Courtesy Montana Historical Society. 43—Untitled sketch, William Cary, copied by Oliver Willcox, courtesy The Thomas Gilcrease Institute of American History and Art, Tulsa, Oklahoma. 44,45—Courtesy Rare Book Division, The New York Public Library, Astor, Lenox and Tilden Foundations. 46,47—Paulus Leeser, courtesy Rare Book Division, The New York Public Library, Astor, Lenox and Tilden Foundations. 48 through 51—Courtesy Rare Book Division, The New York Public Library, Astor, Lenox and Tilden Foundations. 52—Courtesy Missouri Historical Society. 55—Courtesy Rare Book Division, The New York Public Library, Astor, Lenox and Tilden Foundations. 56,57—Courtesy Missouri Historical Society. 58—Courtesy Rare Book Division, The New York Public Library, Astor, Lenox and Tilden Foundations. 61—Courtesy Missouri Historical Society. 62—Courtesy The New York Public Library, Astor, Lenox and Tilden Foundations. 65—Courtesy Missouri Historical Society. 66—Courtesy Risvold Collection, Minneapolis. 67—Courtesy Missouri Historical Society. 68,69—Courtesy Rare Book Division, The New York Public Library, Astor, Lenox and Tilden Foundations. 71—Courtesy Department of Rare Books and Special Collections, Public Library of Cincinnati and Hamilton County. 72—*Cree Chief Le Tout Pique and Fur Company Agents at Fort Union,* Rudolph Friedrich Kurz, copied by Oliver Willcox, courtesy The Thomas Gilcrease Institute of American History and Art, Tulsa, Oklahoma. 75—Throbeck, courtesy State Historical Society of North Dakota, Bismarck, N.D. 76,77—*The Wood Boat,* George Caleb Bingham, copied by John Savage, courtesy The St. Louis Art Museum. 78,79—*Raftmen Playing Cards,* George Caleb Bingham, copied by John Savage, courtesy The St. Louis Art Museum. 80,81—*Watching The Cargo,* George Caleb Bingham, courtesy The State Historical So-

234

ciety of Missouri. 82,83 — David F. Barry, courtesy Montana Historical Society. 84,85 — E. E. Henry, from the Collection of David R. Phillips. 86,87 — Courtesy Department of Rare Books and Special Collections, Public Library of Cincinnati and Hamilton County. 88 — John Savage, courtesy St. Louis Mercantile Library Association. 90,91 — Courtesy Missouri Historical Society. 93 — Courtesy Risvold Collection, Minneapolis. 94 — Courtesy Smithsonian Institution, Museum of History and Technology, Photo No. 72-7890. 96 through 99 — Drawings by John Fryant. 100 — Courtesy Risvold Collection, Minneapolis. 102,103 — Courtesy J. William Kisinger, Brownsville, Pa. 106,107 — Paulus Leeser, courtesy Rare Book Division, The New York Public Library, Astor, Lenox and Tilden Foundations. 108 — Figure I of U.S. Patent No. 913, by H. M. Shreve, September 12, 1838. 109 — Courtesy The State Historical Society of Missouri. 110 — Courtesy The New York Public Library, Astor, Lenox and Tilden Foundations. 112,113 — L. C. Cooper, courtesy State Historical Society of North Dakota, Bismarck, N.D. 114,115 — Courtesy Missouri Historical Society. 116,117 — Orlando S. Goff, courtesy State Historical Society of North Dakota, Bismarck, N.D. 118,119 — Courtesy St. Louis Public Library. 120,121 — Paulus Leeser, courtesy Rare Book Division, The New York Public Library, Astor, Lenox and Tilden Foundations. 122 — E. E. Henry, from the Collection of David R. Phillips. 124 — Courtesy Montana Historical Society. 125 — Courtesy Smithsonian Institution, National Anthropological Archives, Photo No. 2856-53. 127 — Courtesy Montana Historical Society. 128,129 — F. Jay Haynes, courtesy The Haynes Foundation. 132 — Courtesy Dorothy Blunt Hagen and Dr. James K. Blunt; courtesy The State Historical Society of Missouri. 133 — Courtesy Dorothy Blunt Hagen and Dr. James K. Blunt. 134 — Courtesy Dorothy Blunt Hagen and Dr. James K. Blunt; courtesy State Historical Society of North Dakota, Bismarck, N.D. 135 — Courtesy State Historical Society of North Dakota, Bismarck, N.D. 138,139 — Courtesy Oregon Historical Society. 141 — Courtesy The State Historical Society of Missouri. 142,143 — S. J. Morrow, courtesy State Historical Society of North Dakota, Bismarck, N.D. 144 — Courtesy Oregon Historical Society. 145 — Courtesy Risvold Collection, Minneapolis. 146,147 — Courtesy *The Waterways Journal,* St. Louis, Missouri. 149 — T. C. Power Collection, courtesy Montana Historical Society. 150 — Courtesy Dorothy Blunt Hagen and Dr. James K. Blunt. 152 through 157 — Oliver Willcox, courtesy The Thomas Gilcrease Institute of American History and Art, Tulsa, Oklahoma. 152,153 — *Buffalo Crossing the Missouri,* William Cary. 154,

155 — *The Fire Canoe,* William Cary. 156,157 — *Trading on the Upper Missouri,* William Cary. 158,159 — E. E. Henry, from the Collection of David R. Phillips. 160,161 — Al Lucke Collection, courtesy Montana Historical Society. 162,163 — Courtesy Montana Historical Society. 164,165 — Courtesy State Historical Society of North Dakota, Bismarck, N.D. 166,167 — Courtesy Montana Historical Society. 168 — Lee Corrigan, courtesy Shirley Coulson Walpole. 170 — Courtesy Smithsonian Institution, National Anthropological Archives, Photo No. 3545-A. 172 — Yankton County Historical Society's Dakota Territorial Museum. 174,175 — Tolman, courtesy Nebraska State Historical Society. 176,177 — Courtesy Nebraska State Historical Society. 178,179 — F. Jay Haynes, courtesy The Haynes Foundation. 181 — Mark Edgar Hopkins Hawkes, courtesy the B. Hay Collection. 182 — Courtesy State Historical Society of North Dakota, Bismarck, N.D. 183 — Thomas C. Power, courtesy Montana Historical Society — T. C. Power Collection, courtesy Montana Historical Society. 184 — Courtesy Montana Historical Society — F. Jay Haynes, courtesy The Haynes Foundation. 185 — F. Jay Haynes, courtesy The Haynes Foundation. 187 — Courtesy of the *Annals of Iowa.* 188 through 191 — Courtesy State Historical Society of North Dakota, Bismarck, N.D. 193 — F. Jay Haynes, courtesy The Haynes Foundation. 194 through 199 — Henry Beville, courtesy Library of Congress. 200,201 — F. Jay Haynes, courtesy The Haynes Foundation. 202 — *Roustabouts on the Steamer Far West,* William Cary, copied by Oliver Willcox, courtesy The Thomas Gilcrease Institute of American History and Art, Tulsa, Okla. 204 through 207 — Courtesy State Historical Society of North Dakota, Bismarck, N.D. 208,209 — Courtesy Montana Historical Society. 211 — F. Jay Haynes, courtesy State Historical Society of North Dakota, Bismarck, N.D. and The Haynes Foundation. 212,213 — John T. Pitman, © The James D. Horan Civil War and Western Americana Collection. 214 — Map by Nicholas Fasciano. 216,217 — Courtesy Montana Historical Society, except bottom left, courtesy U.S. Army Engineer Museum, Fort Belvoir, Virginia. 218,219 — Courtesy Montana Historical Society, except top left, courtesy National Archives. 220,221 — Courtesy National Archives. 222,223 — Orlando S. Goff, courtesy State Historical Society of North Dakota, Bismarck, N.D. 226,227 — Courtesy Union Pacific Railroad Historical Museum. 228,229 — F. Jay Haynes, courtesy State Historical Society of North Dakota, Bismarck, N.D. and The Haynes Foundation. 230,231 — F. Jay Haynes, courtesy The Haynes Foundation. 232,233 — David F. Barry, courtesy Dorothy Blunt Hagen and Dr. James K. Blunt.